THERESA
BAUMGÄRTNER

HIGHLAND
HARVEST

COUNTRYSIDE RECIPES AND
INSPIRATION FOR GATHERINGS

tra.publishing

THE SMELLS OF FALL 5

Golden Days
THE JOY OF HARVESTING IN THE GARDEN AND FIELDS 9

FEEL, SMELL, TASTE 11
Why harvesting vegetables is a lesson for all the senses

GOOD COMPANY 25
The historical fruit varieties around my home

WHY SO LATE, GEORGINA 105
On our love for dahlias

A FALL WELCOME 107

Come, Dream with Me
A JOURNEY TO SCOTLAND 127

OH WONDER, DEAR WONDER 139
The migration of wild geese leaves us in awe

GRAND SCENES, VAST LAND 145
Visiting a legendary hotel

THE FABRIC OF OUR DREAMS 183
Fashion in tweed design

FLORAL ART 193
A visit to the Highland Flower School

WELL-DRESSED 201
On the trail of tweed

TWEED GUIDE 206

Frost
A HINT OF WINTER 215

STAR TIME 217
Nature sinks into its winter slumber, and we bring the first evergreen branches into the house

ACKNOWLEDGEMENTS 249
RECIPE INDEXES 252

THE SMELLS OF FALL

The transition from late summer to early fall feels like only a few days, but it's a gradual shift that's almost imperceptible.

This shift becomes clear as I take in the morning view from my window. A thin fog has settled over the landscape, softening the scene. I throw on my wool coat and slip into rubber boots. The air is cool, smelling of damp moss, ripe apples, and quinces. Dahlias and hydrangeas in a vase add a spicy, earthy fragrance. These are scents I love deeply, for they remind me instantly of this wonderful time of year.

This is fall harvest season in the garden and fields. Is there anything better than the taste of a carrot freshly pulled from the earth? And isn't the first sip of apple juice from the local press divine? This is the much-discussed flavor of childhood, and this season offers many opportunities to rediscover or experience it anew. Whether you're digging in the soil or picking fruits, these are joyful moments for the whole family—being outside in and connecting with nature is exciting for all ages.

My children proudly carry their harvest treasures into the kitchen and are eager to help with the cooking. The air fills with the scents of pumpkin soup and freshly baked bread. The first part of this book showcases recipes that make the most of these seasonal ingredients and mark the beginning of the cozy season indoors.

I like to call this time of year "Tweed Time," as its mood fits perfectly with Scotland—a country where, in the fall, the vast landscapes of the Highlands reveal their wild, romantic side. And that's exactly where we will travel next in this book. On the trail of tweed, we visit a weaving mill and learn about this robust, beautiful fabric. The shop Campbell's of Beauly, near Inverness, has been tailoring garments since 1858, and tweed is still made to measure there today. Originally, tweed clothing was designed to protect against Scotland's harsh, damp climate—a perfect fabric for hiking, fishing, hunting, and bird-watching. Today, tweed is worn for many occasions, and in a time when sustainability is a major focus, this durable wool fabric is in high demand once again. We'll also visit other Scottish artisans and celebrate crafts and recipes inspired by the fall season in this wonderful country.

Back home, the days are already noticeably shorter, and the first frost heralds winter. In the kitchen, we brew tea and bake the first batch of delicately crispy shortbread.

I wish you all the joy that comes with discovering, harvesting, and enjoying everything this wonderful time of year has to offer.

Theresa

Golden Days

THE JOY OF HARVESTING
IN THE GARDEN AND FIELDS

FEEL, SMELL, TASTE

Why harvesting vegetables is a lesson for all the senses

There is such a magical atmosphere in the fields during early fall. Everything is still damp from the mist, but the morning sun hints at a mild day ahead. We slip into rubber boots and throw on our gardening jackets. The wheelbarrow holds baskets and harvest knives. In the kitchen garden of our home, squash and pumpkins grow, their dry leaves already signaling the season's end. These include varieties such as Hokkaido (red kuri), butternut, Musquee de Provence, and a newcomer, autumn cup, a deep green pumpkin with a wonderfully sweet aroma.

"Don't cut too short! Each one needs a hand-sized piece of stem so we can store them until winter," I explain to the children. They eagerly get to work, gathering the pumpkins. "This heavy one is our pumpkin king!" they shout gleefully. We place our harvest in the sun, sorted by type. They still need a few days to dry and ripen before we turn them into delicious dishes in the kitchen.

Whether it's harvesting pumpkins, gathering walnuts, or searching for mushrooms, the harvest season is full of wonderful stories. And for those who live in the city, now is the perfect time to venture into the countryside to experience it for themselves.

"Everywhere is wonderland," wrote Ringelnatz in one of his poems. As a child, I often found this wonderland at my grandparents' farm in Baden, Germany, and those experiences left a lasting impression. To me, nature and the rural garden felt like a gigantic, enchanted perfume shop, a place to collect scents that would stay with me forever. When I close my eyes, I can still vividly recall the fragrances of my childhood: the intense sweetness of ripe mirabelle plums from the orchard, the tangy scent of fresh sauerkraut, or the earthy aroma of root vegetables.

Now, in the fall, the abundant vegetable field feels like a piece of the Garden of Eden. We stroll through the rows, admiring the cauliflower, Tuscan black kale, and large heads of Savoy cabbage. Tall sunflowers border the carrot bed. We carefully dig into the loose soil with a garden fork, bringing Nantes carrots to the surface. In that moment, an indescribable fragrance fills the air! We find thick, thin, and even crooked roots, but we take them all. After a quick brushing off of the soil, one especially beautiful carrot is polished against a sleeve and immediately tasted. The result? A small fireworks display of flavors on the palate: sweet, robust, and deeply satisfying.

Pan-Seared Mackerel with Celery-Apple Salad, recipe on page 14 — GOLDEN DAYS

PAN-SEARED MACKEREL WITH CELERY-APPLE SALAD

SMOKED MACKEREL IS A CLASSIC, BUT PAN-SEARED FRESH MACKEREL FILLETS ARE EQUALLY DELICIOUS!

INGREDIENTS FOR 4–6 SERVINGS:

2 medium apples
1 medium celery root (1 pound / 450 g), peeled
Juice of ½ lemon
1 large egg yolk
1 garlic clove, grated
1 heaping teaspoon Dijon mustard
Sea salt
1 cup (200 g) neutral oil
¾ cup (200 g) Greek yogurt
2 fresh mackerel fillets, rinsed and dried
1 tablespoon clarified butter or ghee
¼ cup (50 g) chopped walnuts, for garnish
½ bunch fresh chives, minced, for garnish

SPECIAL EQUIPMENT:
spiralizer; immersion blender

Using the spiralizer, cut the apples and celery root into fine spaghetti strands and drizzle with the lemon juice. Cut the strands into approximately 2.5-inch pieces.

In a tall container, combine the egg yolk, garlic, mustard, and a pinch of salt. Pour in the oil in a fine stream while using the immersion blender to blend the mixture. Once emulsified, stir in the yogurt. In a large bowl, combine the apples and celery with the dressing, and toss to coat.

Cut each mackerel fillet on the diagonal into three pieces. In a large skillet over medium-high heat, melt the clarified butter. Add the mackerel, skin side down, and fry for 3 minutes. Flip and fry 1–2 minutes longer, until the fish is cooked through.

Transfer the fish to plates, and sprinkle with a little sea salt. Add the celery-apple salad to each plate, garnished with walnuts and chives.

APPLE TOFFEE CAKE

WHEN THE FALL WIND BRINGS NEW SHOWERS OVER THE HIGHLANDS,
IT'S TIME TO SETTLE INTO A COZY CAFÉ AND ORDER A SWEET TREAT.
THIS APPLE CAKE IS A FAVORITE.

INGREDIENTS FOR 1 LOAF:

FOR THE BATTER:
12 tablespoons unsalted butter, at room temperature, plus more for greasing
¾ cup (150 g) light brown sugar
2 teaspoons vanilla sugar or granulated sugar
3 large egg yolks
3 large egg whites
Sea salt
1 cup (100 g) ground almonds or almond meal
¾ cup (100 g) spelt flour (whole grain or regular)
Ground Ceylon cinnamon
1 teaspoon baking soda
1 tablespoon baking powder
2 small apples (about 250 g), grated

FOR THE TOPPING:
2 small apples (about 250 g)
1 tablespoon lemon juice
2 tablespoons honey
1½ tablespoons unsalted butter
Powdered sugar

SPECIAL EQUIPMENT:
12-inch (30-cm) loaf pan

Preheat the oven to 350°F (180°C, convection). Grease the loaf pan with butter.

In a large bowl, cream the butter and sugars until light and fluffy. Gradually beat in the egg yolks one at a time.

In a medium bowl, beat the egg whites with a pinch of salt until stiff peaks form.

In a separate medium bowl, combine the ground almonds, spelt flour, a pinch of cinnamon, and the baking soda and baking powder.

With a spatula, carefully fold in ⅓ of the flour mixture, ⅓ of the whipped egg whites, and ⅓ of the grated apples into the butter mixture. Repeat this process twice more with the remaining ingredients until the batter is light and airy.

Pour the batter into the prepared pan and bake for 25 minutes.

While the cake bakes, make the topping: slice the apples about ⅛-inch thick, and drizzle with the lemon juice to prevent browning.

In a small saucepan over low heat, combine the honey and butter, stirring until the butter melts. Add the apple slices to the saucepan and toss gently until glazed.

Remove the cake from the oven and layer the glazed apple slices on top. Return to the oven and bake for an additional 15 minutes.

Test for doneness by inserting a toothpick into the center of the cake. It should come out clean. Allow the cake to cool in the pan, then dust with powdered sugar before serving.

PEAR TART

AMONG OUR FAVORITE PEARS PLANTED IN OUR ORCHARD IS THE "CONFERENCE" VARIETY. THIS SWEET AND SPICY PEAR WAS INTRODUCED BY THE ENGLISH BREEDER THOMAS FRANCIS RIVERS AT A ROYAL HORTICULTURAL SOCIETY CONFERENCE IN 1895.

INGREDIENTS FOR 1 TART:

FOR THE CRUST:
Unsalted butter, at room temperature, for greasing
½ cup (75 g) whole wheat spelt flour
½ cup (75 g) spelt flour (type 630) or all-purpose flour, plus more for dusting
Sea salt
¼ cup (50 g) light raw cane sugar
7 tablespoons cold unsalted butter
1 large egg yolk

FOR THE FILLING:
2 large eggs
Sea salt
¼ cup (50 g) light raw cane sugar
2 teaspoons vanilla sugar or granulated sugar
¼ cup (30 g) spelt flour (type 630) or all-purpose flour
2 tablespoons unsalted butter, melted
½ cup (125 g) crème fraîche
1 tablespoon rum

FOR THE TOPPING:
1 large or 2 small pears
2 tablespoons maple syrup

SPECIAL EQUIPMENT:
11 ½ x 8-inch (29 x 20-cm) rectangular tart pan; dried beans or pie weights

Grease the tart pan with butter. Make the crust. In a large bowl, combine the flours, a pinch of salt, and the sugar. Cut the cold butter into cubes and add to the flour mixture. Work the butter into the flour with your hands until it forms crumbs. Add the egg yolk and quickly knead the mixture into a dough. Roll out the dough on a lightly floured surface and press it into the tart pan, making an edge about ½-inch high all around. Cover the pan and chill for 30 minutes.

Preheat the oven to 350°F (180°C, convection). Poke the dough several times with a fork, line it with parchment paper, and add the dried beans or pie weights. Bake the crust for 10 minutes, then remove the paper and weights. Let the crust cool in the pan.

Make the filling: In a medium bowl, whisk together the eggs, a pinch of salt, both sugars, and the flour. Add the melted butter, crème fraîche, and rum, stirring until smooth.

Slice the pears thinly, keeping the skin on. Remove the core and seeds.

Lower the oven temperature to 320°F (160°C). Pour the filling into the crust and arrange the pear slices on top. Bake the tart for 30–35 minutes, until golden brown. While still hot, brush the tart with the maple syrup. Carefully remove the tart from the pan and let it cool on a wire rack.

GOOD COMPANY

The historical fruit varieties around my home

There are places that instantly bring back memories. The orchard meadow adjacent to my home in Luxemburg, which we named Hazelnut House, is one such place for me. A few years ago, on a whim, I drove out of the city and into the countryside. It was a rainy, dreary afternoon when I first saw the meadow, which has since become a cherished part of our lives. The impression it left on me is hard to describe, but this image comes close: without any warning, the tall, ancient fruit trees crept into my heart during that encounter and have remained there ever since. Walking through the damp grass, I immediately felt a sense of belonging. The rustic, character-filled orchard reminded me of the meadows at my beloved grandfather's farm and the carefree summers spent there as a child.

I often stroll through this part of the garden. With a cup of freshly brewed coffee in hand, I wander to where the tall trees—apples, pears, and plums—form an impressive canopy. Some are slightly bent or crooked, while others have wide, symmetrical crowns. Each tree has its own personality.

Orchard meadows have a long agricultural tradition and shape our cultural landscape. In the past, nearly every farm had a kitchen garden for vegetables, herbs, and flowers, as well as a meadow with fruit trees. Farmers always cultivated a selection of varieties that suited the local climate and soil conditions.

Today, orchard meadows are valued for their biodiversity and as a source of unique, historical fruit flavors. Many municipalities and organizations are working hard to preserve and maintain these valuable habitats through new plantings and care programs.

At Hazelnut House, the orchard trees also hold a piece of European cultural history. Among the fine company of trees, the Königliche Renette is particularly noteworthy. This variety was once described as the best table apple in a pomological table from 1867. For our Christmas festivities, we polish the small red apples of the Purpurroter Cousinot until they shine. Recently, we also planted the robust regional variety Luxemburger Triumph, a finely aromatic apple that was discovered by chance in the mid-nineteenth century in Junglinster, Luxembourg.

FALL APPLE TART

DURING APPLE HARVEST SEASON,
A TART FRESH FROM THE OVEN IS A MUST!

INGREDIENTS FOR 1 TART:

Unsalted butter, at room temperature, for greasing
6–7 apples (1 ¾ pounds / 750 g)
Juice of ½ lemon
1 cup (100 g) ground almonds or hazelnuts
⅓ cup (70 g) light raw cane sugar
¾ cup (100 g) spelt flour (type 630) or all-purpose flour, plus more for dusting
Sea salt
Ground Ceylon cinnamon
7 tablespoons cold unsalted butter

FOR FINISHING:
2 tablespoons quince or apple jelly

SPECIAL EQUIPMENT:
11-inch (28-cm) round tart pan

Grease the tart pan with butter. Quarter and core the apples, then slice them thinly. Place in a bowl and toss with the lemon juice to prevent browning.

In a large bowl, combine the almonds, sugar, flour, and a pinch each of salt and cinnamon. Cut the cold butter into cubes and add to the bowl. Work in the butter with your hands until it forms crumbs. Knead the mixture into a smooth dough.

Roll out the dough on a lightly floured surface until it is a little larger than the tart pan. Lay the dough in the pan, forming an edge ½-inch high. If desired, press a pattern into the edge using a fork.

Preheat the oven to 350°F (180°C, convection). Toss the apple slices in the lemon juice to prevent them from browning and then arrange the apple slices in an overlapping shingle pattern on the dough. Bake the tart in the hot oven for about 30 minutes, until golden brown.

Warm the jelly in a small pot and brush it over the hot tart.

Tip: Serve the tart slightly warm with a bit of whipped cream.

APPLE CARAMEL CHEESECAKE

THIS RECIPE IS A HEAVENLY OPTION FOR FALL COFFEE BREAKS.

INGREDIENTS FOR 1 CHEESECAKE:

FOR THE CRUST:

1 ⅓ cups (200 g) spelt flour (type 630) or all-purpose flour
¾ cup (100 g) ground almonds
1 teaspoon baking powder
Sea salt
½ cup (100 g) light raw cane sugar
12 tablespoons cold unsalted butter
1 large egg
Unsalted butter, at room temperature, for greasing

FOR THE CHEESECAKE FILLING:

16 ounces (500 g) cream cheese
3 large eggs
¼ cup (50 g) light raw cane sugar
2 teaspoons vanilla sugar or granulated sugar
Sea salt
Zest of 1 lemon
1 tablespoon lemon juice

FOR THE APPLE FILLING:

2 ¼ pounds (1 kg) apples
2 tablespoons lemon juice
3 tablespoons granulated sugar
¾ cup (200 ml) heavy cream
¾ cup (100 g) coarsely chopped walnuts
1 tablespoon cornstarch
1 teaspoon ground Ceylon cinnamon

FOR THE CRUMBLE TOPPING:

1 ¼ cups (150 g) spelt flour (type 630) or all-purpose flour
5 tablespoons cold unsalted butter, diced
⅓ cup (75 g) light raw cane sugar
Sea salt

SPECIAL EQUIPMENT:

10-inch (26-cm) round springform pan

Make the crust: In a large bowl, mix the flour, ground almonds, baking powder, a pinch of salt, and the sugar. Cut the cold butter into small pieces and add to the bowl. Work in the butter with your hands until it forms crumbs. Add the egg and knead the mixture into a smooth dough. Grease the springform pan and press the dough evenly into the bottom, forming a 2-inch-high edge. Poke the crust several times with a fork, then cool for 10 minutes in the freezer or 30 minutes in the fridge. Preheat the oven to 350°F (180°C, convection) and bake the crust for 10 minutes. Let cool slightly.

While the crust bakes, make the cheesecake filling: Mix the cream cheese, eggs, sugars, a pinch of salt, and the lemon zest and juice briefly until smooth. Pour the mixture over the parbaked crust and bake for 30 minutes.

While the cheesecake bakes, make the apple filling: Peel and core the apples, and then cut into 1-inch cubes. Drizzle with the lemon juice. In a medium saucepan, combine the sugar and 2 tablespoons of water. Place over medium heat until the sugar caramelizes, then whisk in the cream. Stir in the walnuts and simmer for 3 minutes. Fold the apples into the caramel sauce and simmer for 5 minutes, or until softened. Stir in the cornstarch and cinnamon and bring to a boil. Remove from heat and set aside.

Make the crumble topping: In a small bowl, combine the flour and butter. Work in the butter with your hands until it forms crumbs, then mix in the sugar and a pinch of salt. Using your fingertips, gently shape the crumbs into small clusters.

Remove the cheesecake from the oven and evenly distribute the caramelized apples on top. Sprinkle the crumble mixture over the apples. Return to the oven and bake for an additional 30 minutes. Allow the cheesecake to cool completely in the pan before removing and serving.

VANILLA BUTTER BRIOCHE

THE SECRET TO THIS LIGHT AND AIRY BRIOCHE IS THE WAY THE BUTTER IS INCORPORATED; IT'S SIMILAR TO A PUFF PASTRY TECHNIQUE.

INGREDIENTS FOR 1 LOAF:

FOR THE DOUGH:
½ ounce (15 g) fresh yeast
⅓ cup (90 g) whole milk, warmed
2 large eggs, lightly beaten
2 ½ cups (300 g) spelt flour (type 630) or all-purpose flour, plus more for shaping
2 tablespoons light raw cane sugar
1 teaspoon sea salt
2 tablespoons unsalted butter, at room temperature, plus more for greasing

FOR THE VANILLA BUTTER:
12 tablespoons unsalted butter, at room temperature
1 vanilla bean

FOR BRUSHING:
1 large egg
2 tablespoons light raw cane sugar

SPECIAL EQUIPMENT:
stand mixer; rolling pin; 12-inch (30-cm) loaf pan

Make the dough: Crumble the yeast into the bowl of a stand mixer fitted with the dough hook. Add the milk and eggs. Add the flour, sugar, and salt, and knead for 3–4 minutes on low speed. Increase the speed to medium and knead for another 5–6 minutes, gradually adding the butter, until the dough is smooth. Cover the bowl and let the dough rise for 1 ½ hours at room temperature.

Once the dough has risen, move it to a work surface and knead it briefly by hand. Place in a bowl, cover, and let it rest in the fridge for at least 2 hours or overnight.

Make the vanilla butter: Place the butter on a plate or in a shallow bowl. Slice the vanilla bean lengthwise and scrape out the seeds with the tip of a paring knife. Mix the seeds into the butter. Transfer the butter to a sheet of parchment paper and shape the butter into a 5-inch square. Fold the parchment paper over to enclose the butter. If necessary, use a rolling pin to spread the butter evenly. Chill the butter in the fridge for at least 1 ½ hours, or overnight.

Remove the dough and the butter from the fridge. Roll the dough into a 10 x 5-inch rectangle. Place the butter square in the middle of the dough and fold the sides of the dough over the butter to cover it completely. Roll out the dough into a long rectangle (about 15 inches long) without widening it too much. Fold ⅓ of the dough inward and then fold the other side over it to create three layers. Press the edges together. Wrap the dough in parchment paper and chill for 30 minutes. Repeat the rolling and folding process one more time, then chill the dough again for 30 minutes.

While the dough chills, grease the loaf pan with butter. Divide the dough in half, then divide each half again then shape into five equal pieces. Roll each piece into a ball with floured hands. Place the dough balls side by side in the prepared loaf pan (2 columns of 5 balls each). Cover the pan and let the dough rise for another 1 ½ hours at room temperature.

Preheat the oven to 350°F (180°C, convection). Lightly beat the egg and brush it over the risen brioche. Bake the brioche for 30 minutes, until golden brown.

While the brioche bakes, make a sugar syrup by combining the sugar and 2 tablespoons of water in a small saucepan. Bring to a boil, stirring to dissolve the sugar. When the brioche comes out of the oven, immediately brush it with the syrup. Let the brioche cool completely before serving.

ROSE HIP JELLY

THIS PRECIOUS JELLY IS MADE FROM THE UNEXPECTED FRUIT OF WILD ROSES!
REMOVING THE SEEDS FROM THE ROSE HIPS TAKES SOME PATIENCE,
BUT WITH TEAMWORK, IT WORKS PERFECTLY.

INGREDIENTS FOR ABOUT 6 JARS:

---

1 ⅛ pounds (500 g) rose hips, washed, stem and blossom ends trimmed
Juice of 1 lemon, divided
Juice of ½ orange
½ vanilla bean
Gelling sugar

SPECIAL EQUIPMENT:
6 twist-off jars, 5 ½ ounces / 160 ml each, sterilized

Halve the rose hips and use a spoon to remove the seeds and the tiny hairs inside. Collect the cleaned rose hip halves in a bowl.

Weigh the rose hip halves and add 1.5 times their weight in water to a medium non-aluminum lidded pot. (For example, if you have 400 g cleaned rose hips, you would add 600 g water to the pot.) Add the rose hips to the pot. In a liquid measuring cup, combine half the lemon juice and all the orange juice. You should have ⅓ cup liquid. If you have less than that, add water to make up the difference. Add this liquid to the pot. Split the vanilla bean lengthwise, scrape out the seeds with the tip of a paring knife, and add both the seeds and pod to the pot.

Cook the rose hips and liquid over low heat with the lid on for 45–60 minutes, or until soft.

Remove the vanilla pod and use a fork or potato masher to mash the rose hips. Strain the mixture in a sieve set over a bowl. Add the remaining lemon juice. Pour into a liquid measuring cup.

Measure out the gelling sugar (you will need ¼ cup gelling sugar per ½ cup rose hip liquid). In a medium non-aluminum saucepan, combine the gelling sugar and rose hip liquid and bring to a boil, stirring constantly. Boil for 4 minutes.

Immediately pour the jelly into the prepared jars, sealing them tightly.

QUINCE-ORANGE JAM

IN THE GARDEN AT HAZELNUT HOUSE, WE HAVE A SPLENDID QUINCE TREE. THE COMBINATION OF QUINCE WITH ORANGE AND VANILLA WAS SOMETHING I FIRST TASTED IN FRANCE AND IMMEDIATELY FELL IN LOVE WITH. THIS JAM ISN'T OVERLY SWEET AND TASTES WONDERFUL WITH YOGURT.

INGREDIENTS FOR ABOUT 8 JARS:

1 ¼ pounds (600 g) quinces
14 ounces (400 g) oranges
1 cup (200 g) gelling sugar
Seeds from 1 vanilla bean

SPECIAL EQUIPMENT:
immersion blender; 8 twist-off jars, 5 ½ ounces / 160 ml each, sterilized

Peel, quarter, core, and dice the quinces. Peel the oranges, ensuring all the white pith is removed, then chop the segments.

Place the quince and orange pieces in a medium lidded pot. Add 1 ¼ cups (300 ml) water, cover, and cook over low heat until soft.

Once the fruit pieces are tender, use the immersion blender to purée them. Add the gelling sugar and vanilla seeds, stirring thoroughly.

Bring the mixture to a boil, then let it simmer for 4 minutes, stirring.

Immediately pour the jam into the prepared jars, sealing them tightly.

RED ONIONS IN PUFF PASTRY

SLOWLY BRAISING ONIONS BRINGS OUT THEIR DELICATE SWEETNESS, MAKING THESE LITTLE PASTRIES IRRESISTIBLE.

INGREDIENTS FOR 12 PASTRIES:

---

6 small red onions
4 tablespoons olive oil, divided
1 tablespoon honey
Sea salt
Leaves from 1 bunch fresh thyme, divided
1 sheet ready-made butter puff pastry (about 10 ounces / 280 g)
Spelt flour (type 630) or all-purpose flour, for dusting
1 large egg
1 tablespoon whole milk
Freshly grated nutmeg
Freshly ground black pepper

Preheat the oven to 350°F (180°C, convection). Peel and halve the onions lengthwise. Coat the bottom of a large baking dish with 2 tablespoons of the olive oil, then arrange the onion halves cut side up. Drizzle with the remaining olive oil and the honey, and sprinkle with 1 teaspoon salt and half the thyme leaves.

Cover the dish with a lid or foil and bake for about 50 minutes, until the onions are tender.

Meanwhile, roll out the puff pastry on a lightly floured surface and use a glass or pastry cutter to cut out 12 circles, each about 3 inches in diameter. Line a baking sheet with parchment paper.

In a small bowl, whisk together the egg, milk, and a pinch each of nutmeg, salt, and pepper.

Remove the onions from the oven. Brush each pastry circle with the egg mixture, place one onion half (cut side up) in the center, and fold the pastry around it. Twist the pastry on two opposite sides to create a decorative shape.

Arrange the pastries on the prepared baking sheet. Pour the remaining egg mixture over the onions and sprinkle with the rest of the thyme leaves.

Bake the pastries for about 20 minutes, until golden brown. Serve warm.

STAMP WORKSHOP

VISITING SCOTTISH WOOLEN MILLS INSPIRED US TO CREATE THIS DESIGN PROJECT. SINCE STAMPING IS SO MUCH FUN, WE ALSO EXPERIMENTED WITH ONION PRINTS. ENJOY THIS LITTLE PRINTING WORKSHOP!

MATERIALS NEEDED:

---

1 roll of hemp cord
1 small empty box with lid
    (e.g., a matchbox)
Scissors
Tubes of water-based acrylic paint
Shallow dishes or plates (for paint)
Flat synthetic bristle brush
A4 or letter-sized drawing paper,
    or packing paper
Cloth for dabbing the brush
Onions of different sizes
Kitchen knife

FOR THE WORKSPACE:
Packing paper or newspaper
Masking tape

TO PROTECT CLOTHING:
Painting apron or smock

Before starting the print workshop, cover the workspace with packing paper or newspaper and secure it with masking tape. While acrylic paints can be washed out, it's still a good idea to wear an apron or smock.

For the string stamp, wrap the hemp cord once around the box and tie a knot to secure it. Continue wrapping the cord parallel around the box, ensuring there's a small gap between the threads. Cut the cord at the end and tie another knot. Test the paint consistency by placing some paint in a dish and thinning it with water if needed. Apply the paint to the stamp with a brush, and press it evenly onto the paper. (Try stamping on a piece of scrap paper before creating patterns on the drawing paper.)

For the onion print, halve the onions and apply paint to the cut surface. Stamp various patterns on the paper and allow it to dry thoroughly.

Tip: The stamping technique offers countless possibilities. You can experiment with fall leaves or vegetable, and larger pieces of stamped packing paper work wonderfully as gift wrap.

LEEK QUICHE

QUICHE IS ONE OF OUR FAVORITE DISHES TO MAKE WITH FRESHLY HARVESTED FALL LEEKS. IT'S ALSO EASY TO PREPARE AHEAD OF TIME AND CAN BE QUICKLY REHEATED IN THE OVEN.

INGREDIENTS FOR 1 TART:

FOR THE DOUGH:
Unsalted butter, at room temperature, for greasing
2 cups (250 g) spelt flour (type 630) or all-purpose flour, plus more for dusting
1 teaspoon sea salt
9 tablespoons cold unsalted butter
2 tablespoons ice water
1 large egg yolk

FOR THE FILLING:
2 large leeks
2 tablespoons olive oil
1 ⅔ cups (400 ml) heavy cream
2 large eggs
1 large egg white
Freshly grated nutmeg
Sea salt and freshly ground black pepper
¾ cup (100 g) grated mountain cheese, such as Gruyère

FOR GARNISH:
Fresh thyme leaves

SPECIAL EQUIPMENT:
11-inch (28-cm) round tart pan, or two 4 x 14-inch (10 x 36-cm) rectangular tart pans

Grease the tart pan(s) with butter and lightly dust with spelt flour. In a large bowl, combine the flour and salt. Cut the cold butter into cubes and work it into the flour with your hands until crumbly. Add the ice water and egg yolk, and knead into a smooth dough.

Roll out the dough on a lightly floured surface to about ⅛ inch (3 mm) thickness, into a shape to fit your pan(s). Carefully place the dough into the pan(s), pressing it firmly onto the bottom and sides. Trim any excess dough from the edges and prick the bottom with a fork. Cover and refrigerate for 30 minutes.

Preheat the oven to 350°F (180°C, convection). While the dough chills, trim the ends of the leeks, cut them in half lengthwise, and rinse them under running water to remove grit or dirt. Shake off excess water, then slice them into ¼ inch-thick rings. In a large skillet, warm the olive oil over medium heat. Add the leeks and sauté until translucent.

Bake the dough in the tart pan(s) for 10–15 minutes, until lightly golden. Meanwhile, whisk together the cream, eggs, and egg white, and season with nutmeg, salt, and pepper to taste.

Spread the leeks evenly over the parbaked dough. Pour the cream mixture over the leeks and sprinkle with the grated cheese. Bake for about 30 minutes, until golden brown. Garnish with fresh thyme leaves before serving.

ROASTED LEEKS WITH LENTIL TOPPING

FOR THIS RECIPE, MY GRANDMOTHER'S VINTAGE ROASTING PAN HAS A MOMENT TO SHINE! THE RESULT IS ABSOLUTELY WONDERFUL.

INGREDIENTS FOR 4 SERVINGS:

FOR THE LEEKS:

2 ¼ pounds (1 kg) leeks
4 tablespoons olive oil, divided
1 tablespoon honey
3 garlic cloves, sliced
Sea salt
½ bunch fresh thyme

FOR THE LENTIL TOPPING:

1 cup (200 g) brown or French green lentils
1 small bay leaf
1 shallot
2 large carrots (about 150 g)
3 tablespoons unsalted butter, divided
1 cup (240 ml) vegetable broth
Sea salt and freshly ground black pepper
1 teaspoon ground cumin
2 tablespoons balsamic vinegar
1 teaspoon honey

FOR THE RED WINE SAUCE:

2 tablespoons light raw cane sugar
1 cup (240 ml) red wine, divided
1 tablespoon balsamic vinegar
1 tablespoon honey
Sea salt

SPECIAL EQUIPMENT:
roasting pan

Preheat the oven to 350°F (180°C, convection). Trim the ends of the leeks, cut them in half lengthwise, and rinse under running water to remove grit or dirt. Dry the leeks well. Cut off a 3-inch piece from 1 leek (white part only) and set aside for later use. Grease the bottom of the roasting pan with 1 tablespoon of the olive oil. Arrange the leeks in the roasting pan, and drizzle them with the remaining olive oil and the honey. Scatter the garlic over the leeks and sprinkle with salt to taste. Toss the leeks to coat them with the oil, then top with thyme sprigs. Cover the roasting pan with a lid or foil and bake for 45–50 minutes, until leeks are tender and slightly browned.

While the leeks cook, rinse the lentils under cold water, then place them in a pot with 1 ¾ cups (450 ml) water and the bay leaf. Bring to a boil, then reduce heat and simmer for about 35 minutes, until tender.

While the lentils cook, finely chop the shallot, carrots, and the reserved piece of white leek. In a large skillet over medium heat, melt 2 tablespoons of the butter and then add the shallots. Sauté until translucent, then add the chopped carrots and leeks, along with the lentils. Stir to combine, then add the vegetable broth, scraping the bottom of the skillet with a wooden spoon to deglaze. Add salt and pepper to taste, and the cumin, balsamic vinegar, and honey. Let simmer for 30 minutes, stirring occasionally. Add more salt and vinegar if desired, then stir in the remaining 1 tablespoon of butter.

For the red wine sauce, in a small pot, stir together the sugar and 1 tablespoon of the red wine. Cook over low heat until caramelized. Add the rest of the wine, balsamic vinegar, and honey. Simmer for about 15 minutes, until reduced by ⅓. Season with salt to taste.

Serve the roasted leeks topped with the lentil mixture and drizzled with red wine sauce.

GOLDEN DAYS – *Roasted Leeks with Lentil Topping, recipe on page 47*

HOMEMADE SAUERKRAUT

SAUERKRAUT IS A MUST-HAVE IN THE FALL SEASON. THE KEY TO GREAT SAUERKRAUT IS THE QUALITY OF THE CABBAGE, WHICH CAN VARY IN FLAVOR. I PREFER ORGANIC CABBAGE, AS IT HAS A PARTICULARLY FINE AROMA. YOU CAN EITHER MAKE A LARGE BATCH IN A FERMENTATION CROCK (AVAILABLE ONLINE), OR MAKE A SMALLER AMOUNT TO STORE IN JARS.

INGREDIENTS FOR A 2.6-GALLON (10-LITER) FERMENTATION POT:

22 ½ pounds (10 kg) green cabbage
1 cup (200 g) Himalayan rock salt
10 juniper berries
Caraway seeds (optional)

SPECIAL EQUIPMENT:
2.6-gallon (10-l) fermentation crock with a lid; clean heavy stones for weighing down sauerkraut

Rinse the fermentation crock with hot water and dry it. Clean and halve the cabbages, remove the cores, and slice them finely using a knife or mandoline. Add a 1-inch layer of cabbage to the crock, sprinkle it with a handful of salt, and firmly press it down with a wooden tamper or the end of a non-handled rolling pin. This process breaks down the cell structure, releasing juice, which is essential for fermentation.

After pressing, add a few juniper berries and, if using, a layer of caraway seeds. Repeat the process of adding cabbage, sprinkling with salt, pressing down, and adding juniper berries and caraway until the pot is full. The cabbage should have released enough liquid to cover it. If not, continue to press down until it does, or add salt water to cover it.

Weigh the cabbage down with heavy stones (or a clean jar filled with rocks or pebbles), and place the lid on the fermentation crock. Fill the water seal to ensure airtightness. Let the cabbage ferment for 3–4 weeks at room temperature. Once fermented, the sauerkraut can be taken out as needed.

INGREDIENTS FOR 2 ONE-LITER JARS:

4 ½ pounds (2 kg) green cabbage
3 tablespoons Himalayan rock salt
4 juniper berries
1 tablespoon caraway seeds

SPECIAL EQUIPMENT:
2 jars with lids, 1 quart (950 ml) each

Clean and halve the cabbage, remove the core, and slice it finely using a knife or mandoline. Place the cabbage in a large bowl. Add the salt and massage the cabbage vigorously with your hands until enough liquid is released to cover the cabbage.

Mix in the juniper berries and caraway seeds, if using.

Pack the cabbage tightly into the jars, pressing it down firmly to ensure that the liquid covers the cabbage completely.

Pour any remaining liquid from the bowl into the jars to ensure the cabbage is fully submerged. Seal the jars with lids.

Let the jars sit at room temperature for 5–7 days. Afterward, move them to a cool place (like the fridge). The sauerkraut will be ready to taste in 2–3 weeks.

POTATO DUMPLINGS WITH APPLE SAUERKRAUT

A FRESH BATCH OF POTATO NOODLES IS THE EPITOME OF COMFORT FOOD. MY GRANDMOTHER, WALBURGA, ALWAYS MAKES LARGE PORTIONS BECAUSE EVERYONE IN THE FAMILY LOVES THIS DISH.

INGREDIENTS FOR 4 SERVINGS:

FOR THE DUMPLINGS:
2 ¼ pounds (1 kg) starchy potatoes
Sea salt
3 tablespoons unsalted butter
1 medium yellow onion, peeled and diced
1 piece stale bread, cubed
1 large egg
1 large egg yolk
Freshly grated nutmeg
2 tablespoons spelt flour (type 630) or all-purpose flour, plus more for dusting
1 tablespoon potato starch

FOR THE APPLE SAUERKRAUT:
2 red apples
1 medium red onion
1 tablespoon olive oil
1 tablespoon honey
1 ⅛ pounds (500 g) sauerkraut, drained of liquid
1 ¼ cups (300 ml) unfiltered apple juice
2 bay leaves
8 juniper berries
1 teaspoon caraway seeds
Sea salt and freshly ground black pepper

FOR FRYING:
3 tablespoons unsalted butter
1 tablespoon olive oil

SPECIAL EQUIPMENT:
potato ricer; large nonstick pan

Boil the potatoes in salted water for 20–25 minutes, until tender.

In a large skillet over medium heat, melt the butter in a pan and add the onion, stirring until lightly browned. Add the bread cubes and fry briefly. Remove from the heat and set aside.

Flour a work surface. Drain and peel the potatoes while they are still warm, then press them through a potato ricer onto the floured surface. Form a well in the center of the mashed potatoes and add the egg, egg yolk, a pinch of nutmeg, 2 teaspoons of salt, and the onion-bread mixture. Sprinkle the flour and potato starch on top. Use floured hands to knead everything into a smooth dough.

Shape the dough into a long roll, cut it into small pieces, and shape each piece into finger-long, finger-thick potato dumplings. Bring a large pot of salted water to a boil and cook one test noodle. If it is too soft, add a little more flour to the dough. Cook the dumplings in batches. They are ready when they float to the surface. Drain and set aside.

For the apple sauerkraut, peel, quarter, and core the apples, and slice them thinly. Peel the onion, halve it, and cut into thin half-rings. In a large skillet over medium heat, warm the oil and sauté the onions until translucent. Add the apple slices and honey, and caramelize for about 3 minutes. Stir in the drained sauerkraut and deglaze with the apple juice. Add the bay leaves and juniper berries, and simmer for 10–15 minutes over low heat, stirring occasionally. Add more apple juice if needed. Sprinkle with the caraway seeds and season with salt and pepper to taste.

Fry the dumplings: In a large nonstick pan, melt the butter and add the olive oil. Add the dumplings and fry until golden brown. Serve immediately with apple sauerkraut on the side.

BORSCHT

THIS BEET SOUP IS ESPECIALLY DELICIOUS ON COOL DAYS.

INGREDIENTS FOR 4 SERVINGS:

2 tablespoons olive oil
1 garlic clove, smashed
1 shallot, peeled and thinly sliced
2 medium beets, peeled and quartered
3 carrots, peeled and thinly sliced
5 waxy potatoes, peeled and diced
½ medium green cabbage, cored and sliced thinly
8 cups (2 l) vegetable broth
2 teaspoons sea salt
4 whole cloves
1 bay leaf
3 tablespoons balsamic vinegar

FOR GARNISH:
1 bunch fresh dill, finely chopped
¾ cup crème fraîche

In a large soup pot over medium heat, warm the olive oil and lightly sauté the garlic and shallot. Remove the garlic. Add the beets, carrots, potatoes, and cabbage, and sauté briefly.

Add the vegetable broth, salt, cloves, and bay leaf, and simmer everything for 30–40 minutes, until the vegetables are very tender.

Remove the bay leaf and cloves, stir in the balsamic vinegar, and season with more salt if necessary. Serve in bowls, garnished with chopped dill and a dollop of crème fraîche.

BEET DUMPLINGS WITH BROWN BUTTER

GLAZED WITH A BROWN BUTTER, THESE DUMPLINGS ARE SIMPLY IRRESISTIBLE! I LIKE TO SERVE THEM WITH A MIXED SALAD OF ARUGULA AND OAK LEAF LETTUCE.

INGREDIENTS FOR 4 SERVINGS:

14 ounces (400 g) spelt bread or white bread
1 ⅓ pounds (600 g) red beets, trimmed
Olive oil
½ cup (120 ml) whole milk
8 ½ tablespoons unsalted butter
1 large red onion, minced
2 garlic cloves, minced
Leaves from 7 sprigs of fresh thyme
1 tablespoon balsamic vinegar
7 ounces (200 g) ricotta
2 large eggs
½ cup (60 g) breadcrumbs
1 teaspoon sea salt
Freshly ground black pepper

FOR SERVING:

3 ½ tablespoons unsalted butter
½ cup (50 g) grated Parmesan cheese

Cut the bread into ½-inch cubes and either dry it overnight on a baking sheet or place it in the oven at 120°F (50°C) for 1 hour, turning occasionally.

Place the unpeeled beets in a pot and cover them with water. Then cover the pot with the lid and let them simmer for 1 hour. Drain and rinse the beets with cold water. When beets are cool enough to handle, coat your hands with olive oil (to prevent staining) and rub off the beet skins under cold running water. Grate the peeled beets coarsely on a box grater.

In a medium bowl, combine the milk and the dried bread cubes. Let soak for a few minutes.

In a large saucepan over medium heat, melt the butter and add the onions, garlic, and thyme leaves. Sauté until soft. Add the grated beets and balsamic vinegar and mix well.

In a large bowl, combine the ricotta, eggs, breadcrumbs, soaked bread cubes, and salt. Add the warm beet mixture and mix everything by hand. Add pepper to taste.

With wet hands, form medium-sized dumplings from the dough.

Bring a large pot of salted water to a boil. Lower the dumplings into the water and cook at a low heat until they float to the surface. Then move the dumplings to a baking sheet lined with parchment paper and let them cool.

While dumplings cool, in a small saucepan, melt the 3 ½ tablespoons of butter. Cook over low heat until the butter browns and smells nutty. Remove it from the heat, toss the dumplings in the brown butter, and serve garnished with the Parmesan.

Kale Salad with Baked Goat Cheese, recipe on page 62 – GOLDEN DAYS

KALE SALAD WITH BAKED GOAT CHEESE

IN THE KITCHEN GARDEN AT HAZELNUT HOUSE, WE CULTIVATE DIFFERENT VARIETIES OF KALE. IN ADDITION TO CURLY KALE, THE DARK GREEN KALE CALLED "NERO DI TOSCANA" IS ONE OF OUR FAVORITES.

INGREDIENTS FOR 4 SERVINGS:

---

1 ⅓ pounds (600 g) kale leaves (ribs removed)
8–10 tender chard leaves (with stems)
4 tablespoons olive oil
4 apples
One 4-ounce log goat cheese, cut into 4 slices
4 tablespoons honey, divided
Leaves from 4 sprigs of fresh thyme
5 ⅓ tablespoons unsalted butter
Zest and juice of 2 oranges
Sea salt and freshly ground black pepper

FOR GARNISH:
½ cup coarsely chopped walnuts

Preheat the oven to 400°F (200°C, top heat or grill function). Line a baking sheet with parchment paper.

Wash the kale and chard and shake dry. Remove the chard stems from the leaves and cut the stems into thin slices. Cut the chard and kale leaves into ¾-inch strips. In a large skillet, warm the olive oil over medium heat. Add the chard stems and sauté for 2 minutes, then add the kale and chard leaves, increase the temperature, and pan-fry until crispy on all sides. Then move the kale and chard to a bowl.

Cut a ½-inch slice vertically from the middle of each apple, slightly off-center to avoid the core. Place the 4 slices on the prepared baking sheet and top each slice with 1 piece of goat cheese. Drizzle each apple and cheese stack with 1 ½ teaspoons of honey and sprinkle with thyme leaves. Place the baking sheet in the oven on the top rack, and grill until golden brown.

Cut the rest of the apples into ¼-inch wedges. In a large skillet over medium heat, melt the butter and sauté the wedges until tender. Add the remaining 2 tablespoons of honey and toss to coat. Cook 1 more minute to caramelize the apples. Add the orange zest and juice, then mix in the fried kale and chard. Season with sea salt and pepper to taste.

To serve, arrange the kale-apple mixture on plates, sprinkle with walnuts, and place a grilled apple slice with goat cheese in the center of each plate. Serve warm.

CAULIFLOWER-ALMOND SOUP

A WARM, CREAMY SOUP IS ALWAYS WELCOME AFTER A LONG DAY IN THE GARDEN. THIS ONE CAN BE PREPARED IN ADVANCE.

INGREDIENTS FOR 4–6 SERVINGS:

FOR THE SOUP:
1 medium cauliflower
3 tablespoons olive oil
1 yellow onion, finely chopped
2 garlic cloves, minced
1 stalk celery, diced
½ cup (100 g) ground blanched almonds
2 teaspoons sea salt
1 cup (240 ml) heavy cream
1 teaspoon honey
1 tablespoon lemon juice
Freshly grated nutmeg

FOR THE GARNISH:
2 hard-boiled eggs
3 ½ tablespoons unsalted butter
3 ½ ounces (100 g) blanched almonds, chopped
1 cup (100 g) breadcrumbs
½ bunch flat-leaf parsley, chopped
Sea salt and freshly ground black pepper

SPECIAL EQUIPMENT:
blender or immersion blender

Cut the cauliflower into small florets. Chop the thick cauliflower stalk into small pieces.

In a large pot over medium heat, warm the olive oil and add the onion and garlic. Sauté until translucent. Add the celery, cauliflower, and ground almonds, and briefly sauté.

Pour in 6 cups (1.5 l) of water; it should cover the vegetables. Add the salt, bring to a boil, and reduce the heat to a simmer. Cook for about 20 minutes, until the cauliflower is tender.

While the soup is simmering, make the garnish: Peel and finely chop the hard-boiled eggs. In a medium saucepan over medium heat, melt the butter and lightly toast the almonds and breadcrumbs until golden. Stir in the chopped eggs and parsley, and season with salt and pepper to taste. Set aside.

Add the heavy cream to the soup and use the blender to purée until smooth. Add more water if needed to get to a spoonable texture. Stir in the honey, lemon juice, and a pinch of nutmeg. (If you'd like an extra-smooth texture, pass the soup through a fine sieve, using the back of a ladle to press the mixture through.)

Reheat the soup briefly, then ladle into pre-warmed bowls or cups and garnish with the almond-egg mixture.

64 | GOLDEN DAYS – *Cauliflower-Almond Soup, recipe on page 63*

ROASTED CAULIFLOWER AND POTATOES WITH TAHINI SAUCE

THE TAHINI SAUCE ENHANCES THE DELICIOUS FLAVOR OF THESE VEGETABLE CREATING A RICH AUTUMN DISH.

INGREDIENTS FOR 4–6 SERVINGS:

---

3 ⅓ pounds (1.5 kg) starchy potatoes, peeled
1 medium cauliflower
4 garlic cloves
½ cup olive oil
Zest of 1 lemon
Juice of ½ lemon
1 heaping teaspoon ground cumin
1 teaspoon ground Ceylon cinnamon
1 teaspoon sea salt
Freshly ground black pepper
3 ½ ounces (100 g) almonds
3 ½ ounces (100 g) raisins

FOR THE SAUCE:
½ cup (100 g) cashew butter
½ cup (100 g) tahini
1 tablespoon olive oil
1 large garlic clove
Juice of 1 lemon
1 ½ teaspoons agave syrup
Sea salt
Ground cumin

SPECIAL EQUIPMENT:
immersion blender

Preheat the oven to 350°F (180°C, convection). Cut the potatoes lengthwise into wedges. Cut the cauliflower into small florets. Chop the thick cauliflower stalk into small pieces. Peel the garlic and either press it through a garlic press or finely grate it.

In a large bowl, combine the olive oil, lemon zest and juice, cumin, cinnamon, salt, and a few grinds of pepper. Add the almonds, raisins, potatoes, and cauliflower, and toss everything to coat.

Spread the vegetables evenly on a baking sheet and roast in the oven for 30–40 minutes, until golden and tender.

While the vegetables roast, make the sauce: In a medium bowl, combine the cashew butter, tahini, ⅔ cup (150 ml) of water, and olive oil, and blend with the immersion blender. Peel the garlic and grate it into the sauce. Add the lemon juice and agave syrup. Add salt and cumin to taste. Blend again until smooth.

Serve the roasted vegetables with the tahini sauce on the side.

WHOLE ROASTED CAULIFLOWER

WHEN ROASTED WHOLE, CAULIFLOWER DEVELOPS A WONDERFUL FLAVOR. THIS DISH PAIRS NICELY WITH BASMATI RICE FOR A FILLING VEGETARIAN MAIN COURSE.

INGREDIENTS FOR 4 SERVINGS:

1 medium cauliflower
1 teaspoon vegetable broth powder
½ cup (120 ml) boiling water

FOR THE SPICE PASTE:
2 garlic cloves, minced or pressed
2 tablespoons olive oil
Juice of 1 lemon
1 teaspoon ground coriander
1 teaspoon ground cumin
1 teaspoon sweet paprika
½ teaspoon sea salt
2 tablespoons maple syrup

FOR THE PARSLEY SAUCE:
1 medium shallot, minced
2 garlic cloves, minced
½ bunch flat-leaf parsley, chopped
1 mild red chili pepper, seeded and minced
½ teaspoon sea salt
2 teaspoons honey
½ cup (120 ml) olive oil
3 tablespoons white balsamic vinegar

SPECIAL EQUIPMENT:
cast-iron pot or Dutch oven with lid

Preheat the oven to 340°F (170°C, convection). Trim only the large outer leaves from the cauliflower, leaving the smaller ones intact. Wash the cauliflower and pat dry. Combine the vegetable broth powder and the boiling water in a heatproof bowl and stir until the powder dissolves.

Make the spice paste: In a small bowl, combine the garlic, olive oil, lemon juice, coriander, cumin, paprika, salt, and maple syrup. Stir until smooth, and then rub the paste all over the cauliflower.

Pour the vegetable broth into the pot. Place the cauliflower in the pot and drizzle any remaining paste over it. Cover the pot with a lid and bake for 45 minutes.

Remove the pot from the oven, baste the cauliflower with the cooking liquid, and then return it to the oven without the lid. Roast for another 20 minutes, until golden brown and tender in the center.

While cauliflower roasts, make the parsley sauce: In a medium bowl, stir together the shallot, garlic, parsley, chili pepper, salt, honey, olive oil, and vinegar.

Remove the cauliflower from the oven and transfer it to a serving dish. Cut it into portions and serve with the parsley sauce.

AUTUMN CUP PUMPKIN SOUP

WE ALL LOOK FORWARD TO THE FIRST PUMPKIN SOUP BUBBLING ON THE STOVE; IT FEELS LIKE THE OFFICIAL START OF THE SEASON!

INGREDIENTS FOR 4 SERVINGS:

2 ½ pounds (about 1.2 kg) edible pumpkin or winter squash, such as autumn cup or Hokkaido (red kuri)
5 tablespoons olive oil, divided
½ teaspoon ground coriander
½ teaspoon ground cumin
½ teaspoon sweet paprika
Unpeeled cloves from 1 head of garlic
3 sprigs fresh thyme
2 medium yellow onions, diced
6 cups (1.5 l) vegetable broth
1 tablespoon white balsamic vinegar
Juice of ½ lemon
Sea salt and freshly ground black pepper

FOR THE SPICE MIX:
1 teaspoon fennel seeds
1 teaspoon cumin seeds
1 teaspoon sesame seeds
1 teaspoon sea salt
1 teaspoon fresh thyme leaves

FOR SERVING:
2 tablespoons chopped roasted cashews
½ cup (12 g) torn flat-leaf parsley
2 tablespoons dried unsulfured currants
2 tablespoons crème fraîche

SPECIAL EQUIPMENT:
blender or immersion blender

Preheat the oven to 350°F (180°C, convection). Halve and peel the pumpkin, then remove the seeds with a spoon. Cut the pumpkin into ¾-inch wedges. In a large bowl, combine 3 tablespoons of the olive oil with the coriander, cumin, and paprika. Add the pumpkin wedges, garlic cloves, and thyme, and toss to coat, then spread evenly on a baking sheet.

Roast the pumpkin for 40 minutes, until soft.

While pumpkin roasts, make the spice mix: In a medium dry pan over medium heat, lightly toast the fennel seeds, cumin seeds, and sesame seeds until they color slightly, then let them cool on a plate. Crush the seeds lightly with a mortar or rolling pin, then transfer to a small bowl. Stir in the sea salt and thyme. Set aside.

In a large pot over medium heat, warm the remaining 2 tablespoons of olive oil, then add the onions and sauté until translucent. Add the roasted pumpkin wedges, squeeze out the soft insides of the garlic cloves into the pot, and deglaze with the vegetable broth. Let the soup simmer for 10 minutes, then use the blender or immersion blender to purée until smooth.

Stir in the vinegar and lemon juice, and season to taste with salt and pepper. If the soup is too thick, add a little water.

Ladle the soup into pre-warmed bowls. Garnish each serving with a sprinkling of cashews, parsley, currants, the spice mix, and a dollop of crème fraîche.

"SEPTEMBER MORNING"

In the fog, the world still rests,
The woods and meadows still dreaming:
Soon you will see, when the veil lifts,
The blue sky unobscured,
The autumn-strengthened world
Flowing in warm gold.

EDUARD MÖRIKE
(1804–1875)

CARAMELIZED BUTTERNUT SQUASH TART

A DELIGHTFUL SMALL DISH FOR A COZY FALL EVENING!
IT'S LOVELY PAIRED WITH A GREEN SALAD.

INGREDIENTS FOR 1 TART:

---

2 ¼ pounds (1 kg) butternut squash
1 large red onion
2 tablespoons olive oil, divided
1 teaspoon fresh thyme leaves
6 tablespoons maple syrup, divided
Sea salt and freshly ground black pepper
7 ounces fresh goat cheese, crumbled
12 walnut halves

FOR GARNISH:
Balsamic cream or aged balsamic vinegar
Fresh thyme leaves

SPECIAL EQUIPMENT:
11-inch (28-cm) round tart pan

Preheat the oven to 350°F (180°C, convection). Peel the squash, cut it in half, scoop out and discard the seeds, and cut the halves crosswise into ¼-inch slices. Slice the onion into thin rings. In a large skillet over medium heat, warm 1 tablespoon of the olive oil. Add the squash slices, onion rings, and thyme, and sauté for 5 minutes. Add 3 tablespoons of the maple syrup and continue to cook, stirring continuously, for another 5 minutes, until squash is lightly browned and slightly softened.

Grease the tart pan with the remaining 1 tablespoon of olive oil. Then drizzle the pan with 1 tablespoon of maple syrup. Layer the squash slices and onions (without the cooking liquid) tightly in the pan and press them down flat. Season with a pinch each of sea salt and pepper, and drizzle 1 tablespoon of maple syrup over the top. Bake the tart for 30 minutes.

Remove the tart from the oven. Carefully pour off any excess liquid. Distribute small pieces of goat cheese and the walnut halves on the tart, and drizzle with the remaining 1 tablespoon of maple syrup.

Turn on the broiler, and broil the tart for 1–2 minutes (watching carefully), until the goat cheese is golden brown.

Garnish with balsamic cream and thyme leaves. Serve warm.

PASTA WITH ROASTED BUTTERNUT SQUASH

EVERY YEAR, WE GROW A LOT OF BUTTERNUT SQUASH IN THE KITCHEN GARDEN AT HAZELNUT HOUSE, FOR THIS PASTA.

INGREDIENTS FOR 4 SERVINGS:

---

2 ½ pounds (about 1.2 kg) butternut squash
3 garlic cloves, sliced
1 large yellow onion, sliced
About 30 fresh sage leaves
¼ cup (60 ml) olive oil
1 tablespoon agave syrup or maple syrup
1 teaspoon ground sweet paprika
1 teaspoon sea salt, plus more for pasta water
1 teaspoon ground cumin
½ teaspoon ground Ceylon cinnamon
9 ounces (250 g) dry orzo (or other small pasta)
⅓ cup (50 g) chopped walnuts
⅓ cup (50 g) slivered almonds
1 cup (240 g) ricotta

Preheat the oven to 400°F (200°C, convection). Peel the squash, cut it in half, scoop out and discard the seeds, and cut the halves into ¾-inch cubes.

In a large bowl, combine the squash, garlic, onion, sage, olive oil, agave syrup, paprika, salt, cumin, and cinnamon. Mix well.

Line a baking sheet with parchment paper and spread the squash mixture evenly across the sheet. Roast for 30 minutes, until it's tender and slightly caramelized.

While the squash roasts, cook the pasta in salted boiling water according to package instructions. Drain and return the pasta to the cooking pot.

In a medium dry skillet over medium heat, toast the walnuts and almonds until aromatic. Set aside.

To the pot with the pasta, add half the roasted squash and all the ricotta. Toss gently until well mixed.

Serve the pasta on pre-warmed plates, topped with the remaining roasted squash and garnished with the toasted walnuts and almonds.

BUTTERNUT SQUASH-POTATO GRATIN

CHILDREN LOVE THIS SIMPLE BAKED DISH!

INGREDIENTS FOR 4–6 SERVINGS:

Olive oil
1 medium butternut squash
    (about 2 pounds / 900 g)
1 ¾ pounds (800 g) starchy potatoes
2 garlic cloves, grated
Leaves from 5 sprigs of fresh thyme
1 ¼ cups (300 g) crème fraîche
2 large eggs, lightly beaten
Freshly grated nutmeg
Sea salt and freshly ground black
    pepper
¾ cup (100 g) freshly grated
    Parmesan cheese

SPECIAL EQUIPMENT:

13 x 10-inch (34 x 26-cm) baking dish;
    mandoline

Preheat the oven to 375°F (190°C, convection). Grease the baking dish lightly with olive oil.

Peel the squash, cut it into quarters, and scoop out and discard the seeds. Using a mandoline (or a very sharp knife), slice the squash and potatoes thinly.

In a large bowl, combine the squash and potato slices, garlic, thyme, crème fraîche, eggs, and a pinch each of nutmeg, salt, and pepper. Stir until everything is well combined.

Transfer the vegetable mixture into the greased baking dish. Sprinkle the Parmesan evenly over the top.

Bake for about 40 minutes, until golden brown. Test the squash and potatoes with the tip of a knife; it should go through easily. Let cool slightly before serving.

FOCACCIA WITH POTATOES AND ONIONS

AT THE COZY CAFE BIAGIOTTI IN BEAULY, WE TRIED FOCACCIA WITH POTATOES AND ONIONS AND WERE IMMEDIATELY ENCHANTED BY THE COMBINATION.

INGREDIENTS FOR 6–8 SERVINGS:

FOR THE DOUGH:
Sea salt
¾ pound (330 g) starchy potatoes, peeled and diced
⅓ ounce (10 g) fresh yeast
1 teaspoon honey
1 ¼ cups (300 ml) lukewarm water
About 3 ½ cups (1 pound / 450 g) type 00 pizza flour (or all-purpose flour)
Olive oil

FOR THE TOPPING:
6 ounces (180 g) new potatoes
Olive oil
1 large yellow onion, thinly sliced into rings
Sea salt
3 tablespoons lukewarm water
Leaves from 1 sprig of fresh rosemary

SPECIAL EQUIPMENT:
mandoline; 13 x 10-inch (34 x 26-cm) baking dish

Bring a large pot of salted water to a boil. Add the diced potatoes and cook for 10–15 minutes, until soft. Drain the potatoes, then transfer them to a medium bowl and mash well.

In another medium bowl, stir the yeast and honey into the lukewarm water. In a large bowl, combine the flour and 1 heaping teaspoon of salt. Slowly pour in the yeast-water mixture and then 3 tablespoons of olive oil, mixing until a soft dough forms. Add the mashed potatoes and knead the dough by hand for 10 minutes, until smooth.

Transfer the dough to a lightly oiled large bowl. Cover and let it rise for about 1 ½ hours. Move the dough to a work surface, and perform a stretch and fold: Lift one edge of the dough and fold it over the rest of the dough. Repeat three more times on all sides. Put the dough back in the bowl, cover, and let it rise for another 1 ½ hours. Repeat the stretch and fold process.

While the dough rises, make the topping: Using the mandoline or a very sharp knife, slice the new potatoes very thinly. Bring a medium pot of water to a boil and cook the slices for 5 minutes, then drain and let cool. In a large skillet over medium heat, warm 2 tablespoons of olive oil and add the onion and a large pinch of salt. Sauté for about 10 minutes, until onion rings are softened. Set aside.

After you have done the final stretch and fold on the dough, grease the baking dish with olive oil and line it with parchment paper. Press the dough into the dish, stretching it to the edges, cover, and let it rise for another 2 hours.

Preheat the oven to 430°F (220°C, convection). Use your fingers to gently press dimples into the surface of the dough. In a small bowl, combine the lukewarm water and ¼ teaspoon of salt, and stir to dissolve the salt. Drizzle the salt water over the dough, followed by 1 tablespoon of olive oil.

In a medium bowl, combine the potato slices and 1 tablespoon of olive oil, and toss to coat. Arrange the onions and potatoes evenly atop the dough. Drizzle the rosemary leaves with oil and tuck a few needles into the dough. Sprinkle with sea salt and drizzle with 1 tablespoon of olive oil.

Bake the focaccia for 30–35 minutes, until golden. If the surface remains pale, briefly brown it under the broiler. Serve warm.

Just climb up to the top and you're ready to go: The dried fern leaves are placed tightly together in a wreath of mossy branches. Piece by piece, a floating autumn spectacle emerges in the room.

We create floating autumn wreaths by arranging dried fern leaves and moss-covered branches.

We have found that wooden embroidery hoops work wonderfully as bases for unique floral arrangements. For this version, we wrapped green hemp cord around the center of the hoop, making an anchor to weave dried flowers, fern branches, or other natural finds between the layers of cord as desired.

MUSHROOM AND CHESTNUT PIE

THIS PIE IS PERFECT FOR A FALL PICNIC AND CAN BE PREPARED IN ADVANCE.
WE LIKE TO SERVE IT WITH A GREEN SALAD.

INGREDIENTS FOR 1 PIE:

FOR THE DOUGH:

¾ teaspoon sea salt
1¾ cups (240 g) spelt flour (type 630) or all-purpose flour, divided
12 tablespoons cold unsalted butter, cubed
5 tablespoons ice water

FOR THE FILLING:

1⅓ pounds (600 g) wild, porcini, or crimini mushrooms, cleaned and diced
2 large red onions, finely chopped
2 garlic cloves, minced
½ bunch flat-leaf parsley, chopped
7 ounces (200 g) cooked chestnuts, diced
Freshly grated nutmeg
Freshly ground black pepper
½ teaspoon garam masala
¼ cup (60 ml) olive oil
1 cup (150 g) pitted prunes, finely chopped
1 large egg, lightly beaten
Sea salt

FOR THE PIE EDGE:

About 35 small sage leaves, washed and dried

Make the dough: Place the salt and half the flour in a large bowl. Quickly mix the butter into the flour with your hands until coarse crumbs form. Add the rest of the flour and mix briefly, then add the ice water. Knead everything together until a smooth dough forms. Wrap the dough in plastic wrap, and chill in the fridge for 1 hour.

Preheat the oven to 390°F (200°C, convection).

Make the filling: In a large bowl, combine the mushrooms, onions, garlic, parsley, chestnuts, a large pinch each of nutmeg and pepper, the garam masala, and olive oil. Stir to coat everything with the oil. Spread the mixture on a baking sheet and roast for 20 minutes. Remove from oven and reduce heat to 350°F (180°C).

Grease the springform pan with butter. Remove the dough from the fridge and divide it into 4 even quarters. Roll out one quarter of the dough into an 8-inch (20-cm) circle and fit it into the bottom of the pan, trimming any excess.

Press the sage leaves against the greased sides of the pan, top side facing out.

Roll out another quarter of the dough into a strip about 22 inches (55 cm) long and 3 inches (7 cm) wide. Press it around the pan's sides, securing the sage leaves.

In a medium bowl, combine the roasted mushroom mixture, chopped prunes, and egg. Season with salt to taste, stir to mix, and spoon the filling into the pie shell.

Roll out the third dough quarter into an 8-inch (20-cm) circle and place it over the filling, pressing the edges to secure it. Cut a small hole in the center of the top dough and insert the cinnamon stick as a decorative "chimney."

RECIPE CONTINUES

FOR BRUSHING:
1 large egg yolk
1 tablespoon whole milk

ADDITIONAL:
Unsalted butter, at room temperature, for greasing
Spelt flour (type 630) or all-purpose flour, for dusting
1 cinnamon stick, for venting

SPECIAL EQUIPMENT:
8-inch (20-cm) round springform panbaking dish

Roll out the last quarter of the dough into a strip about 22 inches (55 cm) long and 3 inches (7 cm) wide. Cut into 3 vertical strips, and braid the strips together. Press the braid onto the top edge of the pie. If there is excess dough, cut it into small decorative shapes and place them on the top of the pie.

Make an egg wash by whisking together the egg yolk and milk, and brush the top of the pie with it. Bake for about 45 minutes, until golden brown. Serve slightly warm.

FALL MUSHROOM PIZZA

WHEN THIS PIZZA COMES OUT OF THE OVEN, CRISPY AND FRAGRANT, WE DRIZZLE IT WITH A LITTLE BALSAMIC REDUCTION FOR THE PERFECT FINISH.

INGREDIENTS FOR TWO 10-INCH / 26-CM PIZZAS:

FOR THE DOUGH:
- ⅓ ounce (10 g) fresh yeast
- 1 teaspoon light raw cane sugar
- ¾ cup (200 g) lukewarm water
- 12 ounces (375 g) type 00 pizza flour (or all-purpose flour), plus more for dusting
- 1 ½ teaspoons sea salt
- 2 tablespoons olive oil

FOR THE TOPPING:
- 6 tablespoons olive oil
- 9 ounces (260 g) porcini or chanterelle mushrooms (or a mix), cleaned and sliced
- 2 garlic cloves, minced
- 2 teaspoons balsamic vinegar
- Sea salt and freshly ground black pepper
- 7 tablespoons (100 g) crème fraîche

FOR THE BALSAMIC REDUCTION:
- ⅓ cup (70 ml) balsamic vinegar
- 1 tablespoon honey

FOR GARNISH:
- Leaves from 2 sprigs of fresh thyme

Make the dough: In a small bowl, dissolve the yeast and sugar in the water. In a large bowl, combine the flour and salt, then pour in the yeast mixture and olive oil. Knead the dough until smooth, then cover and let rise in a warm place for about 2 hours and 15 minutes, stretching and folding twice, once at 45 minutes and once at 1 ½ hours (see page 86 for stretch and fold directions).

Line 2 baking sheets with parchment paper. Divide the dough in half and roll out each half into a 10-inch (26-cm) circle on a lightly floured surface. Move to the baking sheets, cover with a kitchen towel, and let rest 20 minutes. While the dough rests, preheat the oven to 480°F (250°C, convection).

In a large skillet over medium heat, warm the olive oil and add the mushrooms and garlic. Sauté until softened, 5–10 minutes, then deglaze with the balsamic vinegar. Season with salt and pepper to taste.

Spread half the crème fraîche over each pizza, leaving a small border, then distribute the mushroom mixture over the pizzas. Bake for 8–10 minutes, until crispy.

Make the balsamic reduction: While the pizzas bake, combine the balsamic vinegar and honey in a small pot and simmer, stirring continuously, for about 3 minutes.

Drizzle the finished pizzas with the balsamic reduction and garnish with fresh thyme leaves. Serve warm.

Regardless of fashion trends, one can always rely on classic tweed hats in wind and adverse weather.

FALL MUSHROOM SOUP

THIS SOUP IS A DELICIOUS WAY TO WELCOME THE COOLER SEASON!
IT'S ESPECIALLY GOOD SERVED WITH A FRESH BAGUETTE.

INGREDIENTS FOR 4 SERVINGS:

---

2 tablespoons unsalted butter
1 large yellow onion, peeled and finely diced
14 ounces (400 g) crimini mushrooms, cleaned and sliced
2 teaspoons sweet paprika
2 ¾ cups (650 ml) vegetable broth
1 tablespoon soy sauce
2 tablespoons lemon juice
½ cup (100 ml) heavy cream
Sea salt and freshly ground black pepper

FOR GARNISH:
1 tablespoon unsalted butter
1 tablespoon olive oil
A few fresh sage leaves
Optional: grated mountain cheese, like Bergkäse or Gruyère

SPECIAL EQUIPMENT:
blender or immersion blender

In a large pot over medium heat, melt the butter and sauté the onions until they are lightly browned. Set aside a handful of mushrooms for garnish, then add the mushrooms and paprika to the pot and sauté for 5 more minutes.

Add the vegetable broth, stirring to deglaze, then add the soy sauce. Bring to a boil, then reduce to a simmer and cook for 20 minutes.

Stir in the lemon juice and cream, and use the blender to purée until smooth. Season with salt and pepper to taste, and keep warm.

Make the garnish: In a medium skillet over medium-high heat, warm the butter and olive oil. Add the reserved mushroom slices and sage leaves, and pan-fry until the leaves are crispy.

Ladle the soup into pre-warmed bowls and garnish with the fried mushrooms and sage leaves. If desired, sprinkle with grated mountain cheese.

PASTA WITH MUSHROOMS

THIS IS A FAVORITE PASTA DISH, AND IT'S QUICK TO WHIP UP!

INGREDIENTS FOR 2 SERVINGS:

---

14 ounces (400 g) crimini mushrooms, cleaned and sliced
1 large shallot, minced
2 garlic cloves, minced
1 tablespoon olive oil
¼ cup (50 ml) white wine
¼ cup (50 ml) vegetable broth
1 tablespoon soy sauce
1 tablespoon lemon juice
Sea salt and freshly ground black pepper
2 tablespoons unsalted butter
2 tablespoons freshly grated Parmesan cheese
1 bunch flat-leaf parsley, finely chopped
8 ounces (225 g) dried pasta, like tagliatelle or fettucine

FOR GARNISH (OPTIONAL):
Freshly shaved Parmesan cheese

SPECIAL EQUIPMENT:
nonstick pan

In a dry nonstick pan over medium heat, sauté the mushrooms, shallot, and garlic for a few minutes until the mushrooms release their liquid and it evaporates. Add the olive oil and cook briefly.

Pour in the white wine and vegetable broth and simmer for 2 minutes. Stir in the soy sauce, lemon juice, and salt and pepper to taste.

Stir in the butter, grated Parmesan, and parsley.

Meanwhile, cook the pasta in salted boiling water until al dente.

Drain the pasta, reserving ½ cup of the cooking water. Add the pasta to the mushroom mixture and toss to combine. Add some of the cooking water if the sauce needs more liquid. Divide the pasta between pre-warmed plates, garnish with shaved Parmesan if desired, and serve immediately.

WHY SO LATE, GEORGINA?

On our love for dahlias

Our love for dahlias began in the northwest of France. It was market day in the Breton city of Quimper. We were leisurely strolling past the stalls, admiring the variety of fish and buying cheese for a picnic when we came upon a small flower stand. A woman with a low chignon and a colorful apron around her waist was bundling freshly cut flowers from her field—simple bundles without any extra foliage, just pure beauty.

In front of her were velvety, wine-red dahlias. The poet Sarah Kirsch once called this shape "sea urchin dahlias," though a gardener might describe them as cactus dahlias. The friendly market woman sensed our enthusiasm and began telling us about the robustness and incredible blooming capacity of this variety. "And what's the name?" we asked, already mentally searching dahlia catalogs. "It doesn't have a varietal name," she replied. "It's an old, reliable variety from this region," she added, as she handed us the bunches we had requested.

"Madame, would it be possible for you to send us a small tuber of your dahlias in the fall?" we asked hopefully, and we were overjoyed when she nodded in agreement. We quickly jotted down our address, added some money for postage, and said our goodbyes.

Months later, we were puzzled by a slightly crumpled parcel with no return address. When we opened it, we found no letter—just a single dahlia tuber! We were moved to tears, amazed that the market woman had remembered us and sent her Breton dahlia.

When I see those same dahlias bloom in the garden each fall, I often remember that beautiful time in Brittany. By now, they've thrived, and I've cut many blooms for bouquets and fall table decorations. Alongside them bloom other tall and magnificent favorites, like the pale, pastel-colored "Café au Lait" and the large-flowered "Penhill Dark Monarch," whose petals shimmer as though painted with watercolors.

Back in Goethe's time, the dahlia was still known by its old name, Georgina. Near his garden house in Weimar, on the right bank of the Ilm River, the poet is said to have had an impressive collection of dahlias as early as 1814. He loved the fall spectacle of their colors, though he also mentioned the night frosts that abruptly brought the display to an end.

Dahlias originate in Mexico and Central and South America, and they cannot survive the winter in cold climates. After the first frost, we cut their stems down to about a hand's width above the soil. We then dig up the tubers and store them in our cellar in sturdy paper sacks or wooden crates. It's a bit tedious, but well worth the effort. In the spring, we start the tubers in large pots indoors to give them a head start before we transplant them outside at the end of April. At Hazelnut House, we deal with many voles, so we also protect the tubers with wire baskets custom-made from fine-mesh rabbit wire.

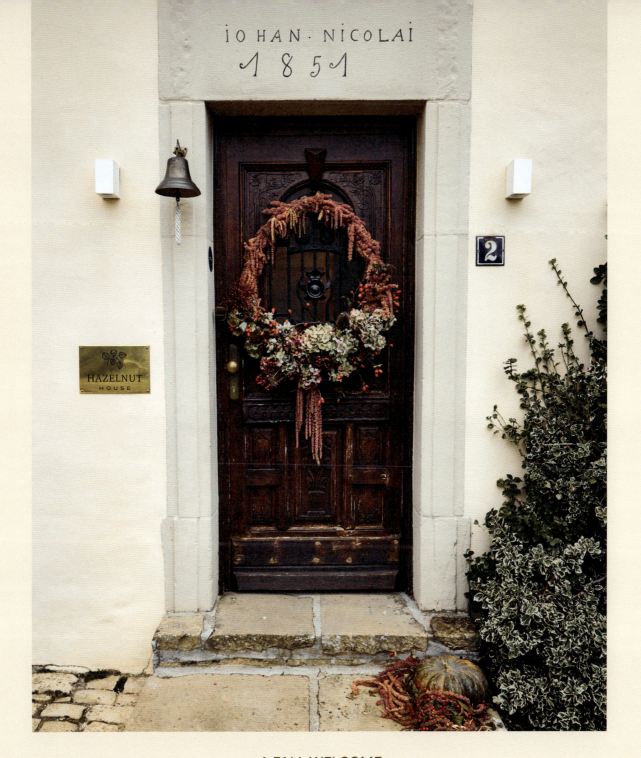

A FALL WELCOME

Don't the long, voluminous flower spikes of the garden foxtail look like precious strands of jewels? In the garden of Hazelnut House, this summer flower from the amaranth family has self-seeded so abundantly that I can also use it for wreaths. For this, I first wrap a willow ring with the flower spikes and secure them tightly with wire, then add hydrangea blooms and rose hip vines.

Fall leaves make charming leaf mobiles. To make one, press the leaves between sheets of paper until they're flat and dry, then dip the leaves in liquid wax and hang them to dry on a line. Use a needle to thread a string through each waxed leaf and tie a knot at the end. Tie the individual strings with the leaves onto a wooden embroidery hoop. Finally, hang the mobile so that the leaves can gently sway in the wind.

"TWEED TIME" BOOKMARK

THIS SEASON IS THE PERFECT TIME TO CURL UP WITH A GOOD BOOK. THIS TWEED BOOKMARK WILL MAKE YOUR EXPERIENCE EXTRA COZY. SIMPLE FOLKLORIC-STYLE MOTIFS SUIT THE TEXTURE OF THE WOOL FABRIC PARTICULARLY WELL. THE STITCHES ARE VERY EASY, AND CRAFTING THIS PROJECT IS WONDERFULLY RELAXING.

YOU WILL NEED:

Ruler
Pencil
Cream-colored A4 or letter-sized cardstock
Utility knife
A small scrap of tweed fabric
Steam iron
Tailor's chalk
Fabric scissors
Embroidery needle
Embroidery thread in various colors

Use the ruler and pencil to draw a 3 ¾-inch (9.5-cm) square on the cardstock. Cut it out with the utility knife.

Iron the tweed fabric using the steam iron. On the fabric, use tailor's chalk to draw a right-angled isosceles triangle with a side length of 3 ¾ inches and cut it out with the fabric scissors.

Embroider simple motifs, such as small trees, onto the fabric using backstitching (Diagram 2). Edge the long side of the triangle with a blanket stitch (Diagram 3) to prevent the fabric from fraying. After embroidering, tie off the threads on the back and steam iron the fabric again briefly.

Place the embroidered fabric triangle exactly onto the cardboard square. Now, use the blanket stitch to attach the fabric to the cardboard (Diagram 1). Done!

1

GOLDEN DAYS | 113

INSTRUCTIONS FOR THE BACKSTITCH:

The backstitch is worked from right to left and consists of evenly spaced stitches. It is mainly used for outlining shapes. First, knot the thread and bring the needle up from the back of the fabric. Insert the needle to the right at a stitch-length distance and bring it back up to the left, twice the stitch-length distance.

For the next stitch, insert the needle into the previous stitch hole, then bring it up again to the left at twice the stitch-length distance. Repeat this rhythm throughout the design.

2

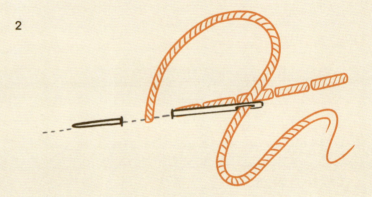

INSTRUCTIONS FOR THE BLANKET STITCH:

The blanket stitch, also known as the festoon stitch, is often usedfor finishing edges. Knot the thread and bring the needle up from the back of the fabric. Insert the needle again from back to front about ⅛ to ³⁄₁₆ inch (4–5 mm) away from the previous stitch. Make sure the needle goes through the loop of the thread before pulling tight. Continue this rhythm to create even loops along the fabric edge.

3

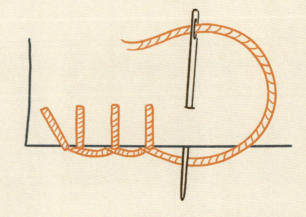

RICE PUDDING WITH CINNAMON-ROASTED FIGS

A COMFORTING TREAT FOR STORMY FALL DAYS!

INGREDIENTS FOR 4 SERVINGS:

FOR THE RICE PUDDING:
1 ¼ cups (250 g) short-grain rice
Sea salt
1 ¼ cups (300 ml) water
1 Ceylon cinnamon stick
1 ⅔ cups (400 ml) coconut milk
Whole milk

FOR THE FIGS:
8 fresh dark-skinned figs
4 tablespoons honey
1 heaping teaspoon ground Ceylon cinnamon
⅓ cup (100 ml) water

FOR GARNISH:
Ground Ceylon cinnamon
Light raw cane sugar

Preheat the oven to 350°F (180°C, convection).

Rinse the rice under cold water. In a medium saucepan over high heat, bring the rice, a pinch of salt, 1 ¼ cups (300 ml) water, and the cinnamon stick to a boil. Reduce heat to low and simmer for 5 minutes.

Add the coconut milk and cook the rice for another 15 minutes, stirring occasionally. If the liquid is absorbed, stir in the milk a few tablespoons at a time until the rice reaches a creamy consistency. Remove the cinnamon stick.

Place the figs in an oven-safe baking dish. Drizzle them with honey and sprinkle with cinnamon. Pour ⅓ cup (100 ml) of water into the dish.

Roast the figs for about 15 minutes, until soft.

To serve, divide the pudding between 4 bowls, sprinkle each with a bit of cinnamon and raw cane sugar, then top each bowl with 2 roasted figs.

FIG CONFIT

THIS AROMATIC FIG CONFIT IS QUICK TO MAKE
AND PAIRS BEAUTIFULLY WITH STRONG CHEESES.

INGREDIENTS FOR 3 JARS:

---

12 fresh medium purple figs, peeled (about 12 ounces / 350 g after peeling)
3 tablespoons balsamic vinegar
¾ cup (150 g) light raw cane sugar
Juice of ½ lemon
¼ cup (60 ml) port wine
2 tablespoons olive oil
Sea salt and freshly ground black pepper
Ground Ceylon cinnamon

SPECIAL EQUIPMENT:
3 twist-off jars, 5 ½ ounces / 160 ml each

Cut the peeled figs into quarters.

In a small pot over low heat, stir together the balsamic vinegar, sugar, and lemon juice. Stir with a wooden spoon until the sugar dissolves.

Add the figs, port, olive oil, and a pinch each of salt, pepper, and cinnamon. Bring to a simmer over low heat and cook for about 25 minutes, until the figs soften.

Lightly mash the figs with a fork to create a coarse purée.
Transfer the fig confit to jars and store in the fridge for up to 3 months.

PLUM TART

LATE-SEASON PLUMS HAVE A SWEET, FULL FLAVOR
THAT MAKES THEM PERFECT FOR A TART.

INGREDIENTS FOR 1 TART:

FOR THE DOUGH:
- 2 cups (250 g) spelt flour (type 630) or all-purpose flour, plus more for dusting and for the pan
- 1½ teaspoons baking powder
- 9 tablespoons cold unsalted butter, plus more for greasing
- ½ teaspoon sea salt
- 2 tablespoons light raw cane sugar
- 3 large egg yolks

FOR THE FILLING:
- 1 tablespoon breadcrumbs
- 1½ pounds (700 g) plums of your choice, pitted and quartered

FOR THE STREUSEL:
- ¾ cup (100 g) spelt flour (type 630) or all-purpose flour
- 4 tablespoons (50 g) cold unsalted butter, diced
- 3 tablespoons light raw cane sugar
- Sea salt

FOR SPRINKLING:
- ⅓ cup (50 g) slivered hazelnuts
- Ground Ceylon cinnamon
- Powdered sugar (optional)

SPECIAL EQUIPMENT:
- 11-inch (28-cm) round tart pan

Sift the flour and baking powder into a large bowl. Using a box grater, grate the cold butter into the flour mixture. Dissolve the salt and sugar in 3 tablespoons water, then add it to the flour mixture along with the egg yolks. Quickly knead by hand to form a smooth dough. Cover with plastic wrap and refrigerate for 1 hour.

Preheat the oven to 355°F (180°C, convection). Grease the tart pan with butter and dust with a little flour. Roll out the dough on a lightly floured surface to a ⅛-inch (2-mm) thickness. Fit the dough into the prepared pan.

Sprinkle the tart base evenly with the breadcrumbs. Arrange the plum halves in a circular pattern on the dough, skin side down.

Make the streusel: In a medium bowl, combine the flour and butter. Rub the butter into the flour to form crumbs, then mix in the sugar and a pinch of salt. Sprinkle the streusel over the plums. Top with slivered hazelnuts and a sprinkle of cinnamon.

Bake the tart for 30–35 minutes, until golden brown. Once cooled, dust with powdered sugar if desired.

PAPIER-MÂCHÉ LANTERNS

WE COLLECTED THE MOST BEAUTIFUL FALL LEAVES DURING A FOREST WALK AND PRESSED AND DRIED THEM AT HOME BEFORE INCORPORATING THEM INTO THESE WHIMSICAL LANTERNS. THIS PROJECT IS A PERFECT FAMILY ACTIVITY FOR A COOL, RAINY WEEKEND.

MATERIALS NEEDED:

Old newspapers
Balloons
Permanent marker
Wallpaper paste
White tissue paper
Pressed fall leaves or flowers
Clothespins
Clothesline, for drying
Wire, for hanging (optional)
Tealights (candles or LED)

Cover the work surface with old newspaper. For each lantern, start by blowing up a balloon to the desired size. Use the permanent marker to mark the opening of the lantern on the balloon (Drawing 1). The opening should be large enough for you to easily fit your hand inside.

Prepare the wallpaper paste according to the instructions. Generally, you will need about 4 tablespoons of paste to 4 cups (1 l) of water. Tear the tissue paper into strips and use the paste to glue several layers of paper around the balloon up to the marked outline (Drawing 2).

Decorate the lantern by gluing leaves or flowers to the tissue paper with the wallpaper paste. Finally, add one more layer of tissue paper over the leaves (they will show through).

Attach a clothespin to the knot of the balloon, and hang the lantern on a clothesline to dry (Drawing 3). Once fully dry, pop the balloon with a needle and pull out the balloon. If desired, attach wire to the top edges for hanging (Drawing 4). Place a tealight inside the lantern. Ta-da!

Come, Dream with Me

A JOURNEY TO SCOTLAND

SCOTLAND, OUR TWEED WONDERLAND

Places to explore, fall in love with, and never forget

EDINBURGH
Our fall journey begins at Edinburgh Airport, heading toward the Highlands. Edinburgh is undoubtedly one of the most beautiful cities in Europe; its charm stays with you forever.

PERTH
The history of this city is closely tied to the River Tay. A bridge with nine arches, built in 1771, spans Scotland's longest river here.

BLAIRGOWRIE
We arrive at Ivybank Lodge. Once a center of linen weaving, the town is now a popular destination for golf, hiking, and fishing. This is the starting point of the famous Snow Road to the north.

BRAEMAR
Afternoon tea at the legendary Fife Arms Hotel comes with an art-viewing experience. The stunning interiors are full of tweed and tartan. Every September, Braemar hosts the Highland Games.

DUNKELD
This charming small town boasts a great atmosphere and unique shops. Enjoy excellent coffee at Aran Bakery.

AVIEMORE
Located on the River Spey, this popular winter sports center offers beautiful views of Cairngorms National Park from the Cairngorm Guest House.

ABERLOUR
At the Knockando Woolmill, visitors can see how wool was once combed, spun, and woven. Aberlour is also known for its whisky distillery.

INVERNESS
In the far north, near Loch Ness and the Highlands, Inverness is home to excellent seafood restaurants like the River House Restaurant on Greig Street.

BEAULY
Since 1858, Campbell's of Beauly has been a royal warrant holder (meaning they've supplied goods to the British royal family), offering tweed fabrics, country fashion, and custom tailoring.

BELLADRUM
The enchanting Wild Gorse Studio, named after the evergreen shrub with bright yellow flowers, offers floral workshops throughout the year.

ABERFELDY
In this romantic town, you'll find the Watermill Bookshop, Gallery & Café, which includes a tearoom and a world of great books. The Glenlyon Tweed Mill, also in Aberfeldy, produces luxe tweed fabrics.

KILLIN
This peaceful village surprises visitors with roaring waterfalls. In the evening, enjoy a cozy meal at The Courie Inn.

CULROSS
Wandering through the narrow streets of this village feels like stepping back in time. Scenes from the TV series *Outlander* were filmed here.

"OH DEER" FINE SCOTTISH SHORTBREAD

THESE DELIGHTFUL DEER-SHAPED COOKIES IMPRESS IN BOTH FLAVOR AND PRESENTATION! THEIR CHOCOLATE-DIPPED ANTLERS ADD A FUN, ELEGANT TOUCH.

INGREDIENTS FOR ABOUT 50 COOKIES:

2 cups (250 g) spelt flour (type 630) or all-purpose flour, plus more for dusting
¼ cup (60 g) light raw cane sugar
1 teaspoon ground Ceylon cinnamon
½ teaspoon ground cardamom
Sea salt
10 ½ tablespoons cold unsalted butter, cubed
1 large egg yolk

FOR DECORATION:
2 ounces (56 g) dark chocolate, melted (or use half white chocolate and half dark chocolate)
1 tablespoon finely chopped almonds

SPECIAL EQUIPMENT:
deer-shaped cookie cutter (or other cookie cutter of your choice)

In a large bowl, combine the flour, sugar, cinnamon, cardamom, and a pinch of salt. Add the butter and rub it into the flour mixture with your hands until it forms coarse crumbs. Add the egg yolk and quickly knead everything into a dough. Cover it with plastic wrap and chill in the fridge for 30 minutes.

Preheat the oven to 320°F (160°C, convection). Line 2 baking sheets with parchment paper. On a lightly floured surface, roll out the dough to a ⅛-inch (3-mm) thickness. Use the cookie cutter to cut out the cookies, and place them on the prepared baking sheets. Reroll and cut any scraps to use all the dough.

Bake the cookies for 14–16 minutes, until light golden brown. Let cool for 1–2 minutes, then transfer to a wire rack to cool completely.

When the cookies are cool, dip the antlers into the chocolate, allow the excess to drip off, and sprinkle with the chopped almonds. Return to the wire rack until the chocolate is completely set.

Store the cookies in an airtight container for up to 1 week.

A cup of freshly brewed tea is an essential part of the "warm welcome" in Scotland.
In the cozy library of the Ivybank Lodge in Blairgowrie, arriving feels like coming home.

"MY HEART'S IN THE HIGHLANDS"
An excerpt

Farewell to the Highlands, farewell to the north,
The birth-place of Valour, the country of Worth;
Wherever I wander, wherever I rove,
The hills of the Highlands for ever I love.

ROBERT BURNS
(1759-1796)

OH WONDER, DEAR WONDER

The migration of wild geese leaves us in awe

It's like a grand outdoor cinema. The fall wind pulls back the curtain of clouds, revealing an endless sky as the screen above us. We tilt our heads back, shading our eyes with our hands. Loud calls announce the show. At first, we can't quite see anything. Searching the skies, we turn in circles until we spot them clearly: wild geese, soaring high above us! Following their familiar rhythm, they are on their way south. There must be hundreds, joined together for this migratory journey. How graceful and beautiful their flight is! In silent awe, we watch these sky dancers bid farewell to colder regions, heading toward warmer lands. At this moment, we are once again reminded of the ancient wisdom nature reveals to us, and the respect with which we should approach it.

The journey of migratory birds has always fascinated people—the timing of their departure, the navigation of precise flight routes, and their return over mountains, seas, and land to their breeding grounds. Much has been studied about this phenomenon, but many mysteries remain.

In the fall, as nature prepares for the coming winter, we are invited to take a closer look. Children love to venture outside as adventurous explorers and curious little scientists. Every glance through binoculars or a magnifying glass fills them with wonder and fascination. There's the vineyard snail, for example, sealing its shell with a chalky lid for winter hibernation. Or the hedgehog, building a cozy nest with leaves and moss for the cold months. The squirrel is busy storing winter supplies, and field mice have tucked seeds and grains into their burrows in the meadow.

These observations can easily inspire fantastical stories, and no one told and illustrated them better than the children's author Beatrix Potter. In the early 1900s, she first shared stories through illustrated letters to children in her family circle. From these letters, beloved classics like *The Tale of Peter Rabbit* and *The Tale of Jemima Puddle-Duck* were born. Perhaps a lesser-known facet of Potter's legacy is her environmental activism—she was deeply committed to the natural conservation of her beloved Lake District. When she passed away, she bequeathed 16 square kilometers of land to the National Trust. Her Hill Top farmhouse, in the English county of Cumbria, was restored and is now open to the public, keeping her memory and her stories alive. One day, we will travel there, for the love of nature connects us all.

"DUNKELD" OVERNIGHT OATS

INSPIRED BY THE CHARMING SCOTTISH TOWN OF DUNKELD, THIS BREAKFAST BOWL FEATURES A TOPPING OF APPLESAUCE, YOGURT, AND GRANOLA.

INGREDIENTS FOR 4 SERVINGS:

FOR THE OVERNIGHT OATS:
½ cup (40 g) rolled oats
¼ cup (50 g) chia seeds
¼ cup (40 g) chopped almonds
¼ cup (40 g) raisins
2 ½ cups (600 ml) whole milk or almond milk

FOR THE GRANOLA:
3 cups (250 g) rolled oats
½ cup (70 g) unsalted sunflower seeds
¼ cup (40 g) flax seeds
1 teaspoon sea salt
1 teaspoon ground Ceylon cinnamon
¼ cup (60 ml) liquid coconut oil
¼ cup (60 ml) honey
½ cup (70 g) hazelnuts
¼ cup (40 g) hemp seeds
½ teaspoon ground ginger
½ teaspoon ground cardamom

FOR THE APPLESAUCE:
2 apples, peeled, cored, and diced
½ cup (100 ml) apple juice, plus more if needed
1 teaspoon ground Ceylon cinnamon
1 tablespoon light raw cane sugar

FOR SERVING:
4 small apples
½ cup (100 g) plain yogurt
¼ cup (50 g) Greek yogurt
Unsweetened coconut flakes

Make the overnight oats: The evening before, combine the oats, chia seeds, almonds, raisins, and milk in a container with a lid. Stir to combine, then cover and refrigerate overnight.

Make the granola: The evening before, preheat the oven to 350°F (180°C, convection). Line a baking sheet with parchment paper. In a large bowl, combine the oats, sunflower seeds, flax seeds, sea salt, and cinnamon. Add the coconut oil and honey, and mix everything with your hands until the dry ingredients are evenly coated. Spread the mixture evenly on the baking sheet and bake for 20 minutes until golden brown, stirring halfway through. Let the granola cool completely.

While granola cools, place the hazelnuts on a baking sheet and toast them in the oven for 10 minutes, until fragrant. Let the hazelnuts cool slightly, then enclose them in a clean kitchen towel and rub until the skins come off. (Some skin may remain; that's fine.) Coarsely chop them, then add them to the cooled granola along with the hemp seeds, ginger, and cardamom. Mix well, then transfer to an airtight container.

Make the applesauce: In a medium saucepan with a lid, combine the apples, apple juice, cinnamon, and sugar. Cover the saucepan with the lid and let the mixture simmer for 20–25 minutes, adding more juice if needed, until the apples are soft. Mash them with a fork to create a chunky applesauce.

In the morning, grate the apples and stir them into the overnight oats along with the plain yogurt. Divide the oats between 4 bowls, and top each with a quarter of the applesauce, 1 tablespoon of Greek yogurt, 1–2 tablespoons of granola, and a handful of coconut flakes.

Tip: Store the remaining granola in an airtight container for up to 3 weeks.

GRAND SCENES, VAST LAND

Visiting a legendary hotel

The pebbles in front of the Victorian house glisten with rain as we arrive at Ivybank Lodge in the evening. Our route from Edinburgh Airport led us through Perth to Blairgowrie. It's only a little over an hour's drive, but the unfamiliar left-hand-side driving and relentless rain proved quite challenging. But, by the next morning, while enjoying a warming Highland porridge, we quickly forget the arduous journey. Gary, our Scottish host, serves a fine breakfast tea along with his personal travel tips. "Here in Blairgowrie is the starting point for the Snow Roads Scenic Route. It passes along the eastern part of the Cairngorms National Park, and it's breathtakingly beautiful," he shares with great enthusiasm. We could listen to his lively descriptions for hours, but it's time to move on. As we drive through the gate, he waves one last time. Scottish hospitality is truly heartwarming—it wraps around you like a soft woolen blanket in this rugged land.

The day seems to greet us with open arms. The wild, dramatic landscape on either side of the road leaves us silent, in awe of its vast beauty. The moorlands glow in warm fall hues, as if someone had rolled Persian rugs down the mountains. On the barren stretches, we spot small groups of Scottish Blackface sheep, a hardy and resilient breed. Pheasants, adorned in vibrant plumage, flap their wings before disappearing into the tall ferns. You can't help but feel the urge to reach for a sketchbook or grab binoculars for spontaneous exploration. The Highlands have always been a place of magical inspiration, as reflected in the writings of Sir Walter Scott, Robert Louis Stevenson, Robert Burns, and many others.

A sign announces the village of Braemar, nestled along the upper reaches of the River Dee, which is one of Scotland's premier salmon waters. In 1848, Queen Victoria visited the area and was so captivated by it that she decided to return every summer to "Royal Deeside." Balmoral Castle, purchased and renovated, became the royal family's summer residence. It was the best promotion the region could have asked for, soon attracting other British aristocrats and sparking a tourism boom.

In the center of Braemar is The Fife Arms, the famed Victorian hotel. It has experienced many ups and downs, and in recent years it had fallen into disrepair. But its salvation arrived when Swiss gallerists Iwan and Manuela Wirth took over and renovated, reopening the hotel at the end of 2018.

"You must stop by for afternoon tea," Gary had suggested, without going into further detail. As we finally stand in front of the hotel, we have only vague expectations of what awaits us. Upon entering the lobby, we immediately know—a grand dream has come true here! It's a symbiosis between world-class art and Scottish culture at its finest. The Fife Arms houses approximately sixteen thousand antiques, collectibles, and works of art. It sounds overwhelming, but everything is curated so well that it fits magically into the Victorian structure.

There are forty-six unique guest rooms, including the Artist's Studio, a room inspired by the Bloomsbury Group, featuring artistically designed furniture. The Nature and Poetry Rooms tell stories of how the Scottish landscape has influenced craftsmanship and literature. Each room bears the signature of renowned London interior designer Russell Sage, whose touch brings everything into harmony.

In the Drawing Room, the walls are covered with a green-blue tartan, a fabric designed for the hotel by Edinburgh-based designer Araminta Campbell. "I've set up the Royal Earl Grey here, near the fireplace, with a view of the Picasso painting," says a friendly voice. It's Emma Weber, a hotel employee originally from Germany. She shares fascinating stories about the hotel, and we could listen to her for hours. "A real highlight of the year isn't just the Highland Games," she adds, "but also Robert Burns Night, which we celebrate very stylishly here in Braemar." Nat Evans, the hotel's florist, enters the room nearly unnoticed, carrying an armful of fall branches and flowers. With sure but playful hands, she arranges everything beautifully. "Nature right outside our door is my constant source of inspiration," she says with a smile.

The Fife Arms is undoubtedly a Scottish luxury hotel par excellence, but the Wirths have created a welcoming atmosphere that is rare in this category. Everyone is welcome here, and at the attached pub, The Flying Stag, locals and visitors—whether hikers or fishers—mingle. Portraits of Braemar's locals hang on the walls, drawn by Gideon Summerfield, a graduate of the Royal Drawing School in London.

Outside, dusk begins to settle. A man in tweed trousers and a vest tends to the fireplace, carefully stoking the flames until they roar back to life.

OATIES

IN SCOTLAND, OATS AREN'T JUST FOR OATMEAL—THEY'RE OFTEN USED IN BAKING, TOO. THESE TRADITIONAL OAT COOKIES HAVE A TEXTURE SIMILAR TO SAVORY CRACKERS.

INGREDIENTS FOR ABOUT 30 COOKIES:

---

1 ½ cups (180 g) rolled oats
1 teaspoon light brown raw sugar
Sea salt
Baking soda
¼ cup (65 ml) hot water
3 tablespoons unsalted butter, cubed
Spelt flour (type 630) or all-purpose flour, for dusting

SPECIAL EQUIPMENT:
food processor; round cookie cutter; thin wooden skewer

Use the food processor to grind the oats into a fine meal. In a large bowl, combine the oats, sugar, 2 pinches of salt, and a pinch of baking soda. In a medium bowl, combine the hot water and butter, and whisk until the butter melts. Pour the liquid into the dry ingredients and knead everything by hand into a dough.

Line a baking sheet with parchment paper and preheat the oven to 320°F (160°C, convection). On a lightly floured surface, roll the dough to a 3-mm thickness. Use a round cookie cutter (about 1 ¾ inches / 4.5 cm in diameter) to cut out cookies. If desired, decorate the cookies by using the skewer to poke small holes about 5 mm apart along the edge. Transfer the cookies to the baking sheet and bake for about 20 minutes, flipping them over after 15 minutes, until golden.

Let the cookies cool on a wire rack and store them in an airtight container for up to 1 week.

Tip: Oaties are delicious when paired with a strong cheese, like Stilton, and chutney.

SPICE-CURED SALMON

SCOTTISH SALMON IS KNOWN FOR ITS QUALITY, AND WHEN CURED AT HOME, IT TASTES ABSOLUTELY EXCEPTIONAL.

INGREDIENTS FOR 6–8 SERVINGS:

FOR THE SALMON:
3 pounds (1.5 kg) salmon fillet with skin
1 tablespoon coriander seeds
1 tablespoon black peppercorns
1 tablespoon caraway seeds
1 tablespoon grated fresh ginger
⅓ cup (70 g) light brown raw sugar
¼ cup (70 g) sea salt

FOR THE PICKLED RED CABBAGE:
½ small red cabbage (about 12 ounces / 350 g)
1 small white onion
¼ cup (50 g) light brown raw sugar
1 clove
1 bay leaf
3 juniper berries
½ cup (100 ml) white wine
¼ cup (60 ml) white balsamic vinegar

FOR THE DILL-MUSTARD SAUCE:
1 bunch fresh dill
½ cup (120 g) medium-spicy mustard
½ cup (100 g) light brown raw sugar
6 tablespoons white balsamic vinegar
⅔ cup (150 ml) canola oil

FOR SERVING:
1 lemon
½ bunch fresh dill
1 tablespoon pink peppercorns

SPECIAL EQUIPMENT:
tweezers; spice grinder; immersion blender; salmon knife

Two days before serving: Run your hand over the surface of the salmon to find any remaining bones; use tweezers to remove them. In a small dry skillet over medium heat, toast the coriander, pepper, and caraway seeds until they release their aroma. Let them cool, then grind them coarsely with a mortar and pestle or spice grinder. In a medium bowl, combine the spices, ginger, sugar, and salt. Cut the salmon in half horizontally. Sprinkle the spice mixture generously on the flesh side of both salmon pieces and press to adhere it.

Place one piece of salmon skin-side down in a large dish, then place the second fillet on top, skin-side up, and press down gently. Cover the dish with plastic wrap and weigh it down with a flat plate to press the fillets together. Transfer to the fridge and cure the salmon for 2 days; after the first day, drain the liquid and flip the salmon so the other fillet's skin side is on top.

The day before serving, make the pickled cabbage: Finely shred the red cabbage and place it in a large heatproof bowl. Peel and finely dice the onion. In a small pot over low heat, combine the sugar and 2 tablespoons water and cook, stirring continuously, until the sugar melts. Add the onion, clove, bay leaf, and juniper berries, and let them caramelize briefly. Pour in the wine and vinegar, then let the mixture simmer for 10 minutes. Pour the hot liquid over the cabbage, mix briefly, cover, and let it marinate in the fridge for 1 day, tossing once.

The day of serving, make the dill-mustard sauce: Strip the dill leaves from the thick stems and chop the leaves finely. Set aside. In a tall container, combine the mustard, sugar, vinegar, and oil, and use the immersion blender to blend. Stir in the dill.

Rinse the salmon briefly under cold water, pat them dry, and slice them thinly at an angle using the salmon knife. Arrange the slices on a large plate. Slice the lemon and garnish the salmon with sprigs of dill, pink peppercorns, and lemon slices. Serve with the pickled cabbage and dill-mustard sauce.

Tip: This goes well with Spelt Walnut Bread (page 175).

The bar at The Fife Arms is called Elsa's, named after the unforgettable fashion designer Elsa Schiaparelli. It glows pink as darkness falls over the Highlands.

SCOTTISH NUT ROAST BALLS WITH JEWELED RICE

THE COLORFUL RICE, TOPPED WITH THESE VEGAN NUT ROAST BALLS, MAKES FOR A VISUALLY STUNNING DISH.

INGREDIENTS FOR 4 SERVINGS:

FOR THE NUT ROAST BALLS:
- ⅓ cup (50 g) cashews
- ⅓ cup (50 g) hazelnuts
- ¾ cup (100 g) blanched almonds
- 5 tablespoons olive oil, divided
- 1 small yellow onion, finely chopped
- 1 garlic clove, minced
- 1 small carrot, diced
- 1 stalk celery, diced
- 2 ½ ounces (75 g) crimini mushrooms, diced
- 1 tablespoon fresh thyme leaves
- ½ cup (50 g) panko breadcrumbs
- 1 tablespoon smooth peanut butter
- 3 tablespoons chickpea flour
- ½ teaspoon ground cumin
- ½ teaspoon ground coriander
- Freshly grated nutmeg
- Sea salt

FOR THE RICE:
- 1 teaspoon sea salt
- 1 teaspoon turmeric
- 1 ¼ cups (250 g) basmati rice, rinsed and drained
- 1 tablespoon olive oil
- 2 tablespoons finely chopped pistachios
- ¼ cup (30 g) dried unsulfured currants
- 3 tablespoons pomegranate seeds

FOR THE YOGURT SAUCE:
- 1 ¼ cups (300 g) Greek yogurt
- 1 teaspoon honey
- 1 teaspoon grated lemon zest
- 2 teaspoons olive oil
- Sea salt
- 2 sprigs fresh dill, chopped (optional)

Make the nut roast balls: Combine the cashews, hazelnuts, and almonds in a food processor. Process until finely ground, then transfer them to a large bowl. In a large skillet over medium heat, warm 2 tablespoons of olive oil and sauté the onion and garlic until translucent. Add the carrots, celery, mushrooms, and thyme, and cook for 5 minutes. Let the mixture cool, then combine with the ground nuts. Add the panko, peanut butter, chickpea flour, cumin, coriander, and a pinch each of nutmeg and salt, and knead the mixture by hand until it binds together. Shape it into small balls. In the nonstick pan over medium-high heat, warm 3 tablespoons of olive oil and fry the balls (in batches if necessary) until golden brown. Turn them while frying to make sure they brown evenly without burning. Set aside.

Make the rice: In a medium pot with a lid, bring 2 cups (½ l) of water to a boil. Add the salt and turmeric, and stir in the rice. Reduce the heat to low, cover, and let it simmer for 12–15 minutes. Stir in the olive oil, pistachios, currants, and pomegranate seeds.

Make the yogurt sauce: In a small bowl, combine the yogurt, honey, lemon zest, olive oil, and a pinch of salt. Taste and adjust the seasoning, then stir in fresh dill if desired.

Serve the nut roast balls with the jeweled rice and yogurt sauce.

SPECIAL EQUIPMENT:
food processor; nonstick pan

SALMON WITH A CRUNCHY CRUST AND ROOT MASH

THE UNIQUE COMBINATION OF JERUSALEM ARTICHOKES
AND POTATOES IN THIS MASH MAKES IT TRULY ONE OF A KIND.

INGREDIENTS FOR 4 SERVINGS:

FOR THE ROOT MASH:
1 ⅛ pounds (500 g) Jerusalem artichokes, peeled and cut into large pieces
1 ⅛ pounds (500 g) waxy potatoes, peeled and cut into large pieces
½ lemon
1 teaspoon sea salt
2 heaping tablespoons sour cream
2 teaspoons unsalted butter
Freshly grated nutmeg

FOR THE SALMON:
Olive oil
1 ⅓ pounds (600 g) salmon fillet
Sea salt

FOR THE CRUST:
⅓ cup (50 g) sunflower seeds, finely chopped
⅓ cup (50 g) hazelnuts, finely chopped
⅓ cup (50 g) almonds, finely chopped
Zest of 1 lemon
1–2 splashes of lemon juice
1 tablespoon honey
1 teaspoon freshly grated ginger
2 tablespoons olive oil
Freshly ground black pepper
Sea salt

SPECIAL EQUIPMENT:
potato masher

Make the root mash: Fill a large pot with water and add the Jerusalem artichokes and potatoes. Squeeze in the juice from the lemon half and add the salt. Bring to a boil and cook until the vegetables are tender.

Drain the vegetables and return them to the pot. Add the sour cream and mash the mixture with the potato masher, leaving some small chunks. Stir in the butter and add a pinch of nutmeg. Add more salt to taste, if needed.

Preheat the oven to 350°F (180°C, convection). Grease a large baking dish with olive oil. Rinse the salmon with cold water, pat it dry, and cut it into 4 equal pieces. Place the salmon in the baking dish, skin side down, and sprinkle with sea salt.

Make the crust: In a medium bowl, combine the sunflower seeds, hazelnuts, almonds, lemon zest and juice, honey, ginger, olive oil, and a pinch each of pepper and sea salt. Spread the mixture evenly over the salmon. Bake for about 15 minutes, until the salmon is just cooked through but still slightly pink in the center.

Serve the salmon with the root mash on pre-warmed plates.

PEARS AND BRUSSELS SPROUTS WITH POTATO-CELERY MASH

THE SWEET, FRUITY AROMA OF PEARS PAIRS PERFECTLY WITH THE ROBUST FLAVOR OF BRUSSELS SPROUTS IN THIS DISH.

INGREDIENTS FOR 4 SERVINGS:

FOR THE MASH:
Sea salt
1 ⅛ pounds (500 g) starchy potatoes, peeled and cut into large pieces
1 ⅛ pounds (500 g) celery root, peeled and cut into large pieces
1 tablespoon unsalted butter
1 medium yellow onion, finely chopped
½ cup (125 ml) heavy cream
Freshly grated nutmeg

FOR THE BRUSSELS SPROUTS AND PEARS:
1 ⅛ pounds (500 g) Brussels sprouts, trimmed and halved
¼ cup (60 ml) olive oil
1 shallot, thinly sliced
1 ⅛ pounds (500 g) pears of your choice, peeled, cored, and cut into ¼-inch slices
1 tablespoon honey
1 teaspoon ground Ceylon cinnamon
¾ cup (200 ml) vegetable broth
Juice of 1 orange
Sea salt and freshly ground black pepper

SPECIAL EQUIPMENT:
potato masher

Make the mash: Fill a large pot with salted water and add the potatoes and celery root. Bring to a boil and cook until the vegetables are tender. Remove them from the water with a slotted spoon (do not discard the water) and transfer them to a large bowl. Mash with the potato masher.

In a medium skillet over medium heat, melt the butter and sauté the chopped onion until golden. In a small saucepan, warm the cream slightly. Stir the cream and onions into the mashed vegetables. Add a pinch of nutmeg and season with salt to taste. Keep warm.

In the same pot of salted water, boil the Brussels sprouts until tender, about 8 minutes. Drain, pat dry, and set aside.

In a large skillet over low heat, warm the olive oil and sauté the shallot for 3 minutes. Add the pears, honey, and cinnamon, and cook, stirring continuously, until the pears caramelize. Add the Brussels sprouts and the vegetable broth. Bring to a simmer and cook for 5 minutes, then stir in the orange juice. Season with salt and pepper to taste.

To serve, spread some potato-celery mash onto pre-warmed plates and top with the Brussels sprouts and pears. Drizzle with the cooking liquid.

CHEESE SOUFFLÉ WITH A FRESH FIELD SALAD

A SOUFFLÉ FRESH FROM THE OVEN IS ALWAYS SOMETHING SPECIAL!
SERVE IT WITH A GREEN SALAD FOR A PERFECT PAIRING.

INGREDIENTS FOR 4 SERVINGS:

FOR THE SOUFFLÉ:
- 4 tablespoons unsalted butter, plus more for greasing
- ½ cup (70 g) spelt flour (type 630) or all-purpose flour
- 2 cups (500 ml) whole milk
- 6 large eggs, separated
- ¾ cup (80 g) grated mountain cheese, like Gruyère
- Sea salt and freshly ground black pepper
- Freshly grated nutmeg

FOR THE SALAD:
- 1 small red onion, finely chopped
- 2 tablespoons balsamic vinegar
- 2 teaspoons honey
- Sea salt
- Freshly ground black pepper
- 1 small garlic clove, minced or pressed
- ¼ cup (60 ml) olive oil
- 7 ounces (200 g) spring mix or baby lettuce

SPECIAL EQUIPMENT:
1.5-quart (1.4-l) soufflé dish

Preheat the oven to 350°F (180°C, convection). In a medium saucepan over medium heat, melt the butter. Stir in the flour, cook for 1 minute, then gradually whisk in the milk until you have a smooth mixture. Bring to a brief boil, then reduce the heat and simmer for 2 minutes, stirring constantly. Remove it from the heat and let it cool for 5 minutes. Stir in the egg yolks, the cheese, and a pinch each of salt, pepper, and nutmeg.

Grease the soufflé dish with butter. In a medium bowl, beat the egg whites to firm peaks. Fold ⅓ of the egg whites into the egg yolk mixture to lighten it, then gently fold in the rest of the egg whites. Very gently scrape the soufflé mixture into the prepared dish, taking care not to deflate it. Bake for 30 minutes, until golden brown and risen. Don't be tempted to open the oven door to check!

While the soufflé bakes, bring a small pot of water to a boil. Add the chopped onion and blanch for 30 seconds. Drain and dry. In a salad bowl, combine the vinegar, honey, and a pinch each of sea salt and pepper. Stir in the garlic, and then whisk in the olive oil until the dressing emulsifies. Add the blanched onions and the spring mix and toss to coat.

Serve the hot soufflé with the salad on the side.

FISH & CHIPS

THIS CLASSIC BRITISH DISH COMBINES CRISPY OVEN-BAKED FRIES WITH TENDER, GOLDEN, FRIED FISH FILLETS AND A TANGY HOMEMADE REMOULADE.

INGREDIENTS FOR 4 SERVINGS:

FOR THE CHIPS:
3 pounds (1.5 kg) waxy potatoes
5 tablespoons olive oil
1 teaspoon sea salt

FOR THE REMOULADE:
1 large egg yolk
1 teaspoon Dijon mustard
½ teaspoon honey
Sea salt
3 tablespoons canola oil
2 heaping tablespoons plain yogurt
1 tablespoon pickle brine
1 tablespoon chopped dill
1 medium dill pickle, finely diced

FOR THE FISH:
1 ⅓ pounds (600 g) skinless fish fillets, like cod or haddock
Sea salt
2 tablespoons spelt flour (type 630) or all-purpose flour
1 large egg
½ cup (50 g) breadcrumbs
3 tablespoons olive oil

SPECIAL EQUIPMENT:
nonstick pan

Make the chips: Preheat the oven to 350°F (180°C, convection). Peel and cut the potatoes into sticks ½ inch (2 cm) thick. Soak the potato sticks in boiling water for 10 minutes, then drain and pat them dry. Toss the potatoes with the olive oil and salt, then spread them on a parchment-lined baking sheet. Bake for about 45 minutes, flipping halfway through, until crispy. Keep warm.

Make the remoulade: In a mixing cup, whisk together the egg yolk, mustard, honey, and a large pinch of salt. Slowly drizzle in the canola oil, whisking continuously, until the mixture emulsifies and forms a mayonnaise. Stir in the yogurt, pickle brine, and chopped dill. Add the diced pickle and mix well. Adjust seasoning with more salt or honey as needed.

Cook the fish: Rinse and pat the fish fillets dry. Remove any bones. Lightly salt the fillets and dust them with spelt flour. Whisk the egg in a shallow dish, and place the breadcrumbs in another dish. Dip each fillet into the egg, then into the breadcrumbs, turning to coat them on all sides. Heat the olive oil in a nonstick pan and fry the fillets for 4–5 minutes on each side, adding more oil if necessary, until the fish are golden and crispy.

Tips:
· *To avoid curdling, ensure that all ingredients for the remoulade are at room temperature.*
· *Serve the fish and chips immediately for maximum crispiness.*

After a stroll through the beautiful streets of Dunkeld, it's wonderful to stop by Aran Bakery and savor the moment (and their delicious pastries).

CINNAMON WREATH

THIS DELICIOUS CINNAMON WREATH IS PERFECT FOR A COZY SUNDAY BREAKFAST.

INGREDIENTS FOR 1 WREATH:

FOR THE DOUGH:
- 8 cups (1 kg) spelt flour (type 630) or all-purpose flour, plus more for dusting
- ½ teaspoon sea salt
- 1 ounce (30 g) fresh yeast
- ½ cup (120 g) light raw cane sugar
- 2 ½ cups (600 ml) lukewarm whole milk
- 4 large egg yolks
- 10 tablespoons unsalted butter, at room temperature

FOR THE FILLING:
- 10 tablespoons unsalted butter, at room temperature
- ½ cup (120 g) light raw cane sugar
- 1 tablespoon ground Ceylon cinnamon
- Sea salt

FOR BRUSHING:
- 1 large egg
- 1 tablespoon whole milk

Make the dough: In a large bowl, combine the flour and salt. Crumble the yeast into a small bowl and add the sugar and milk. Stir until the yeast and sugar dissolve. Stir in the egg yolks, then pour everything into the flour mixture and mix to combine. Cut the butter into chunks and scatter them over the mixture, then knead it by hand until a smooth dough forms. Cover the dough with a cloth and let rise at room temperature for 2 hours.

While dough rises, make the filling: In a medium bowl, combine the butter, sugar, cinnamon, and a pinch of salt. Mix with a fork or hand mixer until smooth.

After the dough has risen, knead it again briefly. On a lightly floured surface, roll the dough with your hands into a log about 3 feet (1 m) long, then flatten the strand and roll it out to about 16 inches (40 cm) wide. Spread the filling evenly over the dough. Starting with one of the long edges, roll the dough up tightly, then cut the roll in half lengthwise, exposing the filling.

Line a baking sheet with parchment paper. Twist the 2 pieces around each other to make a rope. Shape the rope into a wreath and press the ends together to form a circle and secure. Transfer it to the baking sheet, cover it with a towel, and let it rise for 1 hour.

Preheat the oven to 350°F (180°C, fan setting). In a small bowl, whisk together the egg and milk, then brush the wreath with the mixture. Bake for 30–35 minutes, until golden brown. Serve warm.

Highland Scones, recipe on page 174 – COME, DREAM WITH ME

HIGHLAND SCONES

FRESHLY BAKED SCONES ARE A STAPLE OF SCOTTISH TEATIME AND ARE DELICIOUS SERVED WITH CLOTTED CREAM AND JAM. THIS VERSION HAS ENCHANTING HINTS OF CARDAMOM AND CINNAMON FOR AN ADDED AROMATIC TOUCH.

INGREDIENTS FOR ABOUT 15 SCONES:

- 8 cups (500 g) spelt flour (type 630) or all-purpose flour, plus more for dusting
- 1 tablespoon baking powder
- ¼ cup (50 g) light raw cane sugar
- 1 teaspoon ground Ceylon cinnamon
- Sea salt
- Ground cardamom
- 9 tablespoons cold unsalted butter, cubed
- 1 cup (260 g) Greek yogurt
- ¼ cup (50 g) raisins

FOR BRUSHING:
1 large egg yolk

SPECIAL EQUIPMENT:
round cookie cutter

In a large bowl, combine the flour, baking powder, sugar, cinnamon, and a pinch each of salt and cardamom. Add the butter and quickly rub it into the dry ingredients with your hands until the mixture resembles coarse crumbs.

Add the yogurt and knead briefly until a dough forms. Cover the bowl and chill the dough in the fridge for 30 minutes.

Preheat the oven to 390°F (200°C, convection) and line a baking sheet with parchment paper.

Divide the dough in half. Knead the raisins into one half, then roll out both halves to a thickness of about 1 ¼ inches (3 cm) on a lightly floured surface. Cut out 2 ¾-inch (7-cm) rounds using a cookie cutter.

Place the rounds on the prepared baking sheet. Knead and re-roll any dough scraps to use all the dough. In a small bowl, whisk together the egg yolk and water and brush the tops of the scones with it.

Bake for 10–15 minutes, until golden brown.

Tip: Freshly baked scones can be frozen while still slightly warm. This way, you always have a batch ready for a spontaneous treat.

SPELT WALNUT BREAD

A SLICE OF THIS FRESHLY BAKED BREAD IS IRRESISTIBLE. THE PATIENCE REQUIRED TO MAINTAIN A SOURDOUGH STARTER PAYS OFF WHEN YOU TAKE THAT FIRST BITE. YOU CAN BUY SOURDOUGH STARTER OR MAKE YOUR OWN; THERE ARE BEGINNER RECIPES AND INSTRUCTIONS ONLINE.

INGREDIENTS FOR 1 LOAF:

FOR THE STARTER:
1 tablespoon active sourdough starter
½ cup (50 g) rye flour (type 1150)
¼ cup (50 ml) water

FOR THE BREAD DOUGH:
1 ¼ cups (150 g) whole spelt flour
4 cups (500 g) spelt flour (type 630) or all-purpose flour, plus more for dusting
½ cup (50 g) rye flour (type 1150)
2 cups (500 ml) water
4 teaspoons sea salt
1 ¼ cups (150 g) roughly chopped walnuts

SPECIAL EQUIPMENT:
oven-safe cast-iron pot with lid; banneton or proofing basket (optional)

Feed the starter: The day before baking, combine the starter, flour, and ¼ cup (50 ml) of water in a 1-quart (950-ml) glass jar. Mix to combine, then cover loosely and let it sit at room temperature overnight.

Make the dough: The next morning, in a large bowl, combine the spelt flours, rye flour, and 2 cups (500 ml) of water. Stir to combine, then cover the mixture with a towel and let it sit for 1 hour. Add the salt, prepared starter, and walnuts. Knead by hand until a smooth dough forms. Cover and let it rest at room temperature for 3 hours.

First fold: After the rest, fold the dough by lifting one edge and folding it over the rest of the dough. Rotate the bowl and repeat, folding the dough in on itself from different angles 3 more times. Cover and let it rest for 3 more hours.

Second fold and proof: After another 3 hours, fold the dough once more. Transfer it to a well-floured banneton or a bowl lined with a heavily floured cloth, and let it rise overnight at room temperature.

The next morning, place the cast-iron pot with its lid in the oven and preheat to 480°F (250°C). Turn the dough out onto a piece of parchment paper and score it with a very sharp knife. Remove the pot from the oven, and carefully place the parchment paper and dough into the hot pot. Replace the lid and return the pot to the oven. Bake for 10 minutes.

Reduce the temperature to 450°F (230°C) and bake for another 30 minutes. Remove the lid and bake for an additional 20 minutes until the crust is deeply golden.

Carefully transfer the bread to a wire rack. Let it cool completely before slicing.

Tip: Using a well-preheated pot helps create a perfectly crispy crust. And while it's tempting to cut into bread warm from the oven, the crumb inside will only set properly if you let it cool fully. Otherwise, your bread may taste gummy.

COME, DREAM WITH ME — *Spelt Walnut Bread, recipe on page 175*

GRAPEFRUIT ROSEMARY ALE

THIS FRUITY, HERBAL, NONALCOHOLIC DRINK IS PERFECT FOR A COZY EVENING BY THE FIRE WITH FRIENDS. CHEERS!

INGREDIENTS FOR 1 DRINK:

2 teaspoons rosemary syrup (see recipe below)
1 ½ ounces (40 ml) grapefruit juice
Ice cubes
2 ounces (60 ml) ginger ale
1 ½ ounces (40 ml) sparkling mineral water

FOR DECORATION:
1 small rosemary sprig
Light raw cane sugar
Strip of orange zest

FOR THE ROSEMARY SYRUP:
2 long sprigs of fresh rosemary
½ cup (100 g) light raw cane sugar

Make the rosemary syrup: Wash the rosemary, remove the needles, and add them to a small pot along with the sugar and ½ cup (100 ml) of water. Bring to a simmer and cook for 10 minutes, stirring occasionally. Let cool.

Make the drink: In a whisky glass, pour in the rosemary syrup, followed by the grapefruit juice. Add ice cubes and top it off with ginger ale and sparkling mineral water.

Lightly moisten the rosemary sprig and roll it in the raw sugar. Garnish the drink with the sugared rosemary sprig and the strip of orange zest.

THE FABRIC OF OUR DREAMS

Fashion in tweed design

Just ten miles west of Inverness, at the mouth of the River Beauly, lies the small Scottish town of the same name. It's a crisp, pleasant fall morning when we arrive in Beauly. After some brief exploration, we find the shop we've been searching for on High Street. Above the entrance is the name Campbell & Co., with the royal coat of arms prominently displayed underneath. We have an appointment with Nicola Sugden, who runs this business, one of Scotland's oldest tweed shops, with her husband John. Campbell's of Beauly, as it's known here in the Highlands, has been in business since 1858.

"When the Campbell family retired after four generations, we took over the shop in 2015," Nicola explains.

At first, it might seem surprising that the couple left their busy lives in London to carry on here, but the call to the Highlands was no coincidence. Nicola grew up in the area, and John's family has a long history in the Scottish textile industry. The story of the shop and its accompanying tailoring workshop continues to unfold. It's a stroke of luck, you might say, as we stand in awe of the neatly stacked bolts of tweed and the beautiful selection of country-style clothing.

Nicola and John take their time with each customer, which is deeply appreciated, and not just by tradition-conscious Scots. When the tailoring workshop reopened in 2019, a very special guest was in attendance: Prince (now King) Charles. "He loves visiting Scotland and has a passion for tweed," Nicola tells us with a smile as she leads us through the store. The old wooden floors creak beneath our feet. We stop often, marveling at the displays and running our fingers over the soft yarns. "The sweaters with Fair Isle patterns are knitted at a workshop in Aberdeenshire, and we develop the designs together. Over here, the tweed knickers, called Plus Twos, are made in our own workshop. Knee-high wool socks and sturdy shoes complete the look," she says.

We can't resist any longer! In no time, we're in one of the dressing rooms, emerging in tweed trousers, standing happily in front of the mirror. How do they feel? The sensation is unique: warm, durable, and comfortable all at once. In our minds, we're already envisioning ourselves strolling joyfully through Scotland's rugged wilderness—after all, that's what tweed clothing was originally made for.

CASTLE COOKIE BOX

COOKIES BECOME BUILDING BLOCKS FOR A CASTLE—A FUN AND
CREATIVE BAKING PROJECT FOR THE WHOLE FAMILY!

MAKES ABOUT 70 COOKIES

INGREDIENTS:
½ teaspoon baking powder
½ cup (60 g) finely ground blanched almonds
¼ cup (50 g) powdered sugar
½ teaspoon ground Ceylon cinnamon
Zest of ½ lemon
Sea salt
9 tablespoons cold unsalted butter, cubed
1 large egg

SPECIAL EQUIPMENT:
Spelt flour for the work surface
Parchment paper for the baking tray
Square, triangle, and other geometric-shaped cookie cutters

In a large bowl, combine the flour, baking powder, ground almonds, sugar, cinnamon, lemon zest, and a pinch of salt. Add the cubed butter, and mix quickly by hand until crumbly. Beat the egg and transfer half of it to the dough mixture (save the other half for another recipe). Knead the dough briefly, cover, and refrigerate for 30 minutes.

Line 2 baking sheets with parchment paper.

Divide the dough in half. Roll out the first half on a lightly floured surface to a ⅛-inch (3–4-mm) thickness. Use the cookie cutters to cut out "building blocks" for the castle. For the middle section, create a paper template as pictured, place it on the dough, and use a small sharp knife to cut out the shape. Roll out and cut the second half of the dough in the same way.

Place the cookies on the prepared baking sheets and refrigerate them for 30 minutes. While the cookies chill, preheat the oven to 320°F (160°C, convection). Bake the cookies for 10–12 minutes, until lightly golden. Let them cool on a wire rack.

Tip: For a charming gift, stack the cookies in a tin and include royal icing for mortar to build the castle!

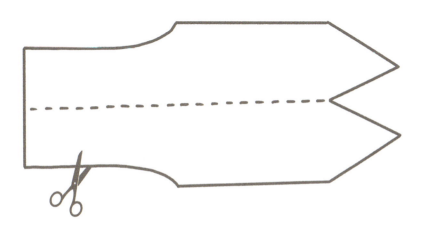

FLORAL ART

A visit to the Highland Flower School

Moss-covered stone walls flank the narrow road leading into Belladrum Estate. The wind-tousled hawthorn and blackthorn hedges line the way to Wild Gorse Studio and the Highland Flower School, nestled in this dramatic and romantic landscape. The name comes from gorse, the vibrant yellow-flowered plant that flourishes along Scotland's coasts.

Julia Kirk, the founder of the studio and of Highland Flower School, greets us with eager anticipation. As she stands on the narrow steps to the studio, her warm, familiar welcome feels as though we're long-lost friends returning after a prolonged absence.

We first discovered her a few years ago in an English magazine. The photo spread captured a Highland wedding, and the moment we saw the pages, it felt like entering a fairytale world. The bridesmaids' floral crowns and bouquets were poetic, natural, and a subtle reflection of Scottish flora. Those images stayed with us, leading us here to meet Julia in person.

Now, as she guides us through her atelier, sunlight pours through the tall glass windows, illuminating the space. Everything is meticulously organized: metal rings of varying sizes hang within easy reach on the walls, alongside an impressive selection of cords and ribbons.

"I've collected these special vessels piece by piece—I love hunting for treasures at flea markets," Julia shares enthusiastically. Just then the door swings open, and we see two young women, Chloe and Catherine, enter, carrying large bundles of ferns smelling of the forest. They spread the ferns on the large worktable and excitedly explain they had been foraging—gathering natural materials from the environment. "Moss, lichen, berries, seed pods, grasses, or branches—fall is such a wonderful time for it," Chloe adds. Catherine had also grown flowers like roses and dahlias herself last season, though most of the cut flowers they use still come from the wholesale market.

Meanwhile, Julia begins arranging dried flowers, rose hips, and seed pods to create a wreath. With what seems like effortless artistry, she blends the different textures of the plants. As the wreath takes shape, she tells us about the journey of the Highland Flower School. When she founded the workshop in 2015, its focus was primarily on floral design for weddings and events. But soon, there was increasing demand for workshops, and today, people from all over the United Kingdom come to learn floral design from Julia.

Meeting and working with other creative flower enthusiasts, she tells us, has always been her dream.

"I've collected these special vessels piece by piece—I love hunting for treasures at flea markets."

JULIA KIRK

WREATH WORKSHOP

Scottish florist Julia Kirk enjoys crafting with natural materials. For her autumn wreath, she uses ferns, grasses, seed pods, and bright-colored straw flowers. The base of the wreath is a thin metal ring. She continually cuts small branches and flowers, bundling them together and wrapping them around the ring with fine wire. Piece by piece, a wreath takes shape, making it easy to replicate in this style.

"HAZELNUT HOUSE" HAZELNUT CAKE

THIS IS A FAVORITE CAKE IN OUR FALL REPERTOIRE—ITS NUTTY FLAVOR AND RICH TEXTURE MAKES IT A SPECIAL TREAT.

INGREDIENTS FOR 1 CAKE:

FOR DECORATING:
1 ounce (30 g) whole hazelnuts
Powdered sugar, for dusting

FOR THE SHORTCRUST PASTRY:
9 tablespoons cold unsalted butter, cubed
1¼ cups (150 g) spelt flour (type 630) or all-purpose flour, plus more for dusting
¼ cup (60 g) light raw cane sugar
½ teaspoon ground Ceylon cinnamon
⅔ cup (75 g) ground hazelnuts
Sea salt

FOR THE FILLING:
2 tablespoons raspberry jam
1 large egg yolk
3 tablespoons light raw cane sugar
1 teaspoon ground Ceylon cinnamon
Sea salt
1 large egg white
⅔ cup (75 g) ground hazelnuts
1 tablespoon breadcrumbs
1 tablespoon spelt flour (type 630) or all-purpose flour
Baking powder
⅓ cup (80 ml) heavy cream

SPECIAL EQUIPMENT:
8-inch (20-cm) round springform pan

Prepare the hazelnuts for decoration: Toast the whole hazelnuts in a dry skillet over medium heat until fragrant, then rub them in a kitchen towel to remove the skins. Cut the nuts in half and set aside.

Make the shortcrust pastry: Line the bottom of the springform pan with a circle of parchment paper. Place the butter in a large bowl. Add the flour, sugar, cinnamon, hazelnuts, and a pinch of salt. Mix with your hands to form coarse crumbs. Knead briefly into a smooth dough ball. Weigh out 7 ounces (200 g) of the dough and set it aside for the top crust. Roll out the rest of the dough on a lightly floured surface and use it to line the pan, forming an edge ½-inch high. Prick the bottom crust a few times with a fork.

Preheat the oven to 350°F (180°C, convection). Spread the raspberry jam evenly over the bottom crust. In a medium bowl, combine the egg yolk, sugar, cinnamon, and a pinch of salt, and beat until creamy using a whisk or hand mixer. In a separate medium bowl, beat the egg white to firm peaks. In another medium bowl, combine the ground hazelnuts, breadcrumbs, flour, and baking powder, then gradually fold it into the egg yolk mixture. Stir in the cream. Finally, gently fold the whipped egg white into the mixture in two portions. Spread the hazelnut mixture evenly over the jam-covered base.

Roll out the reserved dough for the top crust and place it over the filling. Pierce the surface a few times with a fork to make steam vents, then press the edges down with the back of a wooden spoon handle. Arrange the halved hazelnuts close together around the edge of the cake.

Place the cake in the oven and bake for 35–45 minutes, until golden brown. Remove from the oven and allow to cool briefly before removing it from the pan. Let it cool completely on a wire rack. Dust with powdered sugar once cooled and before serving.

Tip: The hazelnut cake develops its full flavor if allowed to rest for a day after baking. It stays fresh for several days.

WELL-DRESSED

On the trail of tweed

"Tweed is one of Scotland's great gifts to the world."
—VIXY RAE, SCOTTISH FASHION DESIGNER

Beauty stretches far across Scotland. Everything is interconnected: the stormy sea and the rugged landscape, the melodies of "Pipes and Drums" and the song of the wind, the wool of the sheep and the traditional weaving mills. Tweed is everywhere, delicately woven into the fabric of Scottish life. We carry this certainty with us on our journey, and it leads us to marvelous places. Aberfeldy, in Highland Perthshire, is one such find. At a glance, it's a picturesque, dreamy market town by the River Tay. The impressive Wade's Bridge, with its five stone arches, spans the river. There's also a well-known whisky distillery and the remarkable Watermill Bookshop, housed in an old watermill once used for milling oats. A few years ago, it was named the best independent bookstore in Britain.

As soon as we step inside Watermill, we're struck by the warmth emanating from the stove on the ground floor. The scents of tea and freshly baked scones fill the air, and towering sandwiches are being carried out of the tiny kitchen. The inviting concept of this historic building immediately wins us over: warm up and indulge first, then head upstairs to the world of books. Once up there, we immerse ourselves, browsing and reading as time in Scotland seems to stand still. The selection of nature guides alone is impressive. Even the small wren, the tiny bird known as the king of the hedgerows, has several books dedicated to it here. And, unsurprisingly, we find a book on tweed—aptly titled *The Art of Tweed*—by designer Vixy Rae.

In a conversation with the bookseller, we learn that there's a tweed mill right in the neighborhood that still produces fabrics. With eager anticipation, we open the large wrought-iron gate of Glenlyon Tweed Mill, established in 1850. The owner, Michael Gates-Fleming, had been very welcoming over the phone about our spontaneous visit. "Nice to meet you!" he now shouts over the rhythmic clatter of looms.

We are deeply impressed! The venerable factory feels like the perfect setting for a period drama, its presence both strong and mysterious. The air smells of machine oil and countless spools of yarn. The weaver, Gordon Hermiston, is wearing ear protection and seems highly focused as he checks the fabric currently being produced. "We specialize in weaving high-quality tweed fabrics that are deeply connected to this region," Michael explains, gesturing toward the carefully organized fabric rolls on the shelves.

Another service they offer is the custom tailoring of tweed garments. This includes hats like the traditional deerstalker, a tweed cap with ear flaps made world-famous by Sherlock Holmes.

In Glenlyon's accompanying tailoring shop, a small collection is crafted from the fabrics. The warm tweed jackets are the perfect choice for venturing outdoors in the rugged climate of Scotland.

TWEED GUIDE

A brief introduction to the fabric

Tweed is a wool fabric made from carded yarns. These yarns are not combed, making them voluminous and often mottled with small knots. Along with tweed, other fabrics like loden and flannel are also woven from these yarns.

The story goes that the word tweed came about by accident in 1826. The Scottish word for twill fabric is tweel, but a London customer misread it as tweed. Perhaps he had the River Tweed in the Scottish Borders in mind at that moment—who knows?

Twill is one of the three fundamental weaving patterns for tweed, alongside plain weave and satin weave. Twill is known for its surface structure of diagonal lines, called twill ribs. The different arrangements of these ribs are what give tweed fabric its pattern. There is an incredible variety of designs. In Scotland, classic tartans are very popular, but herringbone tweed with its fishbone pattern is also a favorite. The English name "houndstooth" refers to the elegant checked pattern.

HARRIS TWEED is a true icon among tweeds. Only handwoven, high-quality tweeds made in the Outer Hebrides of Scotland can legally bear this name. The wool comes from Cheviot and Scottish Blackface sheep. Unlike other tweeds, Harris Tweed uses wool fleece that is dyed before being spun into yarn. This fleece is mixed in specific proportions before it's spun. A weaver produces about eighty to one hundred meters of tweed fabric per week.

Most modern production uses wider looms powered by foot pedals. The fabric is milled, washed, and inspected before it can be officially labeled as Harris Tweed. Clothing or accessories made from this fabric also carry the official label with the protected designation of origin.

ESTATE TWEEDS are tweeds associated with specific Scottish estates. Their colors and patterns were traditionally designed to blend into the local landscape, making them perfect for hunting.

One of the most famous estate tweeds is **BALMORAL TWEED**, introduced during Prince Albert's time. Although you may still hear the dress code "No brown in town," estate tweeds are now worn on many occasions during the colder seasons.

SHETLAND TWEED is woven from the fine, soft wool of Shetland sheep and is ideal for lighter coats and jackets.

DONEGAL TWEED is not from Scotland, but rather, as the name suggests, from County Donegal in northwest Ireland. This popular tweed is characterized by small, colorful flecks known as *neps*.

"We specialize in weaving high-quality tweed fabrics that are deeply connected to this region."

MICHAEL GATES-FLEMING

WEAVING FASCINATION

On a rack, numerous spools of yarn are stored, ready for weaving preparation. The warp threads are visible on the loom, running longitudinally. In the past, water power was used to drive the machines in the weaving mill; today, water wheels are merely relics from a bygone era.

COME, DREAM WITH ME | 207

COME, DREAM WITH ME — *Napkin Ring for a Fall Dinner, instructions on page 210*

NAPKIN RING FOR A FALL DINNER

THESE RUSTIC TWEED NAPKIN RINGS ARE A PERFECT FIT FOR A CASUAL FALL DINNER PARTY—OR FOR JANUARY 25TH, WHEN SCOTS OBSERVE ROBERT BURNS NIGHT IN HONOR OF THE GREAT SCOTTISH WRITER.

MATERIALS NEEDED FOR 1 RING:*

Tweed fabric scraps
Steam iron
Tailor's chalk
Ruler
Fabric scissors
Sewing thread that matches the fabric
Sewing needle
1 horn button, ¾ inch (2 cm) in diameter
Backing, for reinforcement

* Add more fabric and buttons to make multiple rings

Iron the tweed fabric with the steam iron until it's smooth. Using the tailor's chalk and a ruler, draw a rectangle measuring 5 x 8 ½ inches (13 x 22 cm) on the fabric. Cut it out carefully with the scissors.

Fold a ½-inch (1.25-cm) seam allowance on all edges toward the wrong side of the fabric, and iron down the seams using steam (Diagram 1).

Fold the fabric rectangle in half lengthwise, aligning the edges, and iron to set the fold (Diagram 2a). (To prevent the fabric from becoming too thick at the corners, you can trim a small piece from the seam folds at each corner.)

By hand or with a sewing machine, use the mattress stitch (ladder stitch) to sew the edges together so that the stitches remain hidden inside (Diagram 2b).

Once the fabric is sewn, iron it again with steam to flatten the seam. Form a ring by overlapping the ends by 1 ½ inches (3.8 cm). Secure the ring by sewing a horn button through both layers 1 inch (2.5 cm) from the edge (Diagram 3). Go over it twice to ensure the button stays securely in place.

Tip: If you want to create a whole tablescape, additional décor items can easily be found on a walk in nature: feathers, pinecones, or a few green branches.

1

½ inch (1.25 cm)

4 ⅓ inches (11 cm)

7 ¾ inches (20 cm)

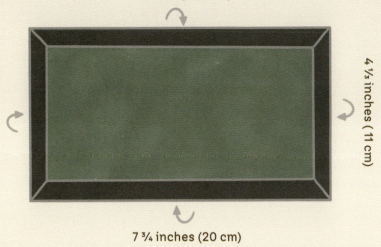

2a

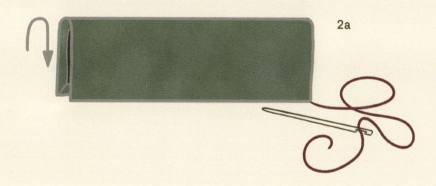

2b

3

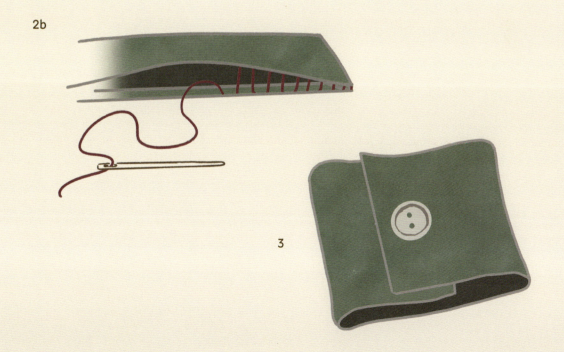

COME, DREAM WITH ME

Freshly collected fall leaves inspire the imagination! How about taking some embroidery thread and a needle to embellish the leaves, just for the fun of it? It brings joy and is wonderfully relaxing.

Frost

A HINT OF WINTER

STAR TIME

Nature sinks into its winter slumber, and we bring the first evergreen branches into the house

It's early on a Sunday morning. The last days of November were gloomy and rainy, but with the new moon, the air has noticeably cooled. Bright light streams through the window, revealing an unexpected, magical transformation outside:
The landscape has been enchanted by frost!
The forest wears a white starry cloak, as if some nature goddess herself had draped it over the
trees overnight. I quickly grab my coat and hat, setting off on a spontaneous morning walk.
Frosty wonders wait for no one!

Just a few minutes later, it feels as if I'm the first visitor to a vast, enchanted park. I'm reminded of the Jardin du Luxembourg, the famous palace garden in Paris. How magical it must be to walk there alone on a winter morning like this. Oh yes, it would surely be peaceful and very still. Waking places have their own poetry, and we can carry a piece of that magic with us into the day.

The glittering all around me, the play of light in the frosted branches—the entire atmosphere today turns my thoughts toward the approaching festive season. Nature's treasures provide beautiful decorations: branches adorned with lichen, dried seed pods, bark covered in moss, or the last rosebuds of the season. The seemingly simple things can be the most convincing. Little finds from nature, like pinecones or feathers, can be arranged into charming still lifes.

What kind of coniferous greenery should it be this season? Maybe a mix? Pine and fir pair well with eucalyptus branches and various herbs. Thick bundles of thyme smell wonderfully aromatic and dry well. And while juniper greenery may be a bit prickly, its blue-green berries are so beautiful. Bringing these green bundles into the house marks the beginning of a heavenly time.

And speaking of heavenly, here's a suggestion: How about gazing at the stars on a clear winter evening? You might even spot the Milky Way and make a secret wish upon a shooting star. Visiting a planetarium is also a perfect addition to your winter wish list. If you find yourself in Europe, consider the Zeiss-Planetarium in Jena, Germany—the oldest planetarium in the world. Visitors have been able to view the stars under its massive dome since 1926.

"Weißt du, wie viel Sternlein stehen an dem blauen Himmelszelt, weißt du, wie viel Wolken gehen weithin über alle Welt?" ("Do you know how
many little stars are in the blue sky? Do you know how many clouds spread all over the world?")
So goes a well-known German children's song by Wilhelm Hey.

I find it comforting to know that we are always accompanied by stars. And isn't this season a beautiful time for stargazing?

"MORNING"

Now the stars are veiled again by pale blue silk,
Now near and far are filled again with the young sun.
Oh, you white waters, tumbling down to the plain,
Tell my friends how my heart sings and resounds today.

CHRISTIAN MORGENSTERN
(1871–1914)

SPICED SHORTBREAD LEAVES

THESE AROMATIC SHORTBREAD COOKIES ARE PERFECT
WITH A WARM CUP OF AFTERNOON TEA.

**INGREDIENTS FOR ABOUT
30 COOKIES:**

9 tablespoons cold unsalted butter, cubed
¼ cup (60 g) light raw cane sugar, plus more for sprinkling
½ cup (60 g) rice flour
1 cup (125 g) spelt flour (type 630) or all-purpose flour, plus more for dusting
½ teaspoon ground cardamom
½ teaspoon ground Ceylon cinnamon
Sea salt

SPECIAL EQUIPMENT:
leaf-shaped cookie cutter

In a large bowl, combine the butter, sugar, rice flour, spelt flour, cardamom, cinnamon, and a pinch of sea salt. Using your hands, mix the ingredients until crumbly. Quickly knead the mixture into a smooth dough, but do not overwork it.

Line 2 baking sheets with parchment paper. On a lightly floured surface, roll out the dough to a ⅛-inch (3-mm) thickness. Slide an offset spatula or long thin knife under the dough to ensure it doesn't stick to the surface. Use the leaf-shaped cookie cutter to cut out the cookies, and place them on the prepared baking sheets.

Use a toothpick to poke small holes along the edges of the leaf-shaped cookies for a decorative touch. Place the baking sheets in the fridge for 30 minutes.

Preheat the oven to 320°F (160°C, convection). Bake the cookies for 13–15 minutes, until they are lightly golden.

While the cookies are still warm, sprinkle them with raw sugar. Transfer them to a wire rack and let them cool completely. Store them in an airtight container for up to 1 week.

HAZELNUT ZWIEBACK

THIS HAZELNUT ZWIEBACK RECIPE IS REMINISCENT OF A NUT BISCOTTI. IT'S PERFECT FOR USING UP LEFTOVER EGG WHITES AND MAKES A CRUNCHY, FLAVORFUL COOKIE THAT STAYS FRESH FOR WEEKS IN AN AIRTIGHT CONTAINER.

INGREDIENTS FOR 1 LOAF:

---

9 tablespoons unsalted butter
6 large egg whites
1 tablespoon vanilla sugar or granulated sugar
½ cup (100 g) light raw cane sugar
1 cup (120 g) spelt flour (type 630) or all-purpose flour
½ cup (80 g) raisins
1 cup (120 g) hazelnuts

SPECIAL EQUIPMENT:
12-inch (30-cm) loaf pan; electric hand mixer

Preheat the oven to 350°F (180°C, convection). Line the loaf pan with parchment paper.

In a small pot over medium heat, melt the butter. In a medium bowl, use the hand mixer to beat the egg whites to firm peaks. Gradually add the vanilla sugar and raw cane sugar to the egg whites, beating continuously until a creamy, pale mixture forms. Gently fold in the spelt flour, raisins, hazelnuts, and melted butter.

Pour the batter into the prepared loaf pan and bake for 30–45 minutes, until a toothpick inserted in the middle of the dough comes out clean. Remove it from the pan and let it cool on a wire rack.

Once the zwieback has cooled, wrap it in plastic wrap and freeze it for 1 ½ hours. Preheat the oven again to 350°F (180°C, convection). Remove the zwieback from the freezer, unwrap it, and let it thaw slightly and then slice them thinly. Line a baking sheet with parchment paper. Bake the slices for 10–15 minutes, until golden brown.

Transfer the zwieback to a wire rack and cool them completely. Store in an airtight container for up to 2 weeks.

MAGICAL FAN GARLAND

THIS ENCHANTING PAPER FAN GARLAND EVOKES IMAGES OF WHITE, FROSTY WINTER FLOWERS OR FAIRYTALE WINGS. IT'S PERFECT FOR DECORATING WINDOWS OR TRANSFORMING SIMPLE BRANCHES INTO FESTIVE DISPLAYS.

MATERIALS NEEDED:

15–20 pieces of translucent white paper or tracing paper, cut into 3 x 4-inch (7.5 x 10-cm) rectangles
Glue stick
Hole puncher
Craft scissors
Thin white thread and needle

Fold your first piece of paper from the shorter side into an accordion, creating folds approximately ⅕ inch (5 mm) wide that alternate back and forth (Drawing 1). Smooth the edges with your fingers as you go.

Fold the accordion in half and glue the halves together (Drawing 2).

Punch a hole in the lower end of the folded fan; this is where the thread will go (Drawing 3).

Cut the two corners of the top edge at an angle to create small points (Drawing 3). Use the hole puncher to punch holes through these points.

Carefully unfold the fan. Thread the white string through the lower holes of your fan and tie a knot to secure them in place (Drawing 4). Repeat with your remaining pieces of paper to create a garland.

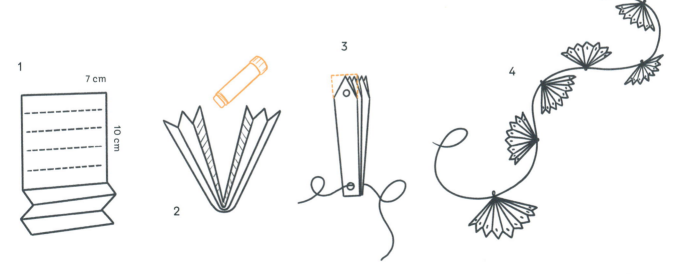

FROST | 225

PAVLOVAS WITH POACHED PEARS

A GORGEOUS PAVLOVA TOPPED WITH WINE-POACHED PEARS IS A STUNNING DESSERT THAT'S PERFECT FOR ANY OCCASION.

INGREDIENTS FOR 4 SERVINGS:

FOR THE PEARS:
¾ cup (180 ml) port wine
1 cup (240 ml) red wine
½ cup (90 g) light raw cane sugar
1 Ceylon cinnamon stick
2 cloves
1 star anise pod
Zest of 3 oranges
4 pears (Conference or Bartlett), peeled and stems left on

FOR THE PAVLOVAS:
2 large egg whites
1 cup (115 g) powdered sugar
1 teaspoon vanilla sugar or granulated sugar
1 teaspoon white balsamic vinegar
1 ½ teaspoons cornstarch

FOR SERVING:
⅔ cup (150 ml) whipped cream
1 tablespoon chopped pistachios

SPECIAL EQUIPMENT:
electric hand mixer

Poach the pears: In a pot large enough to fit the pears, combine the port wine, red wine, 1 cup (240 ml) water, and the sugar, cinnamon, cloves, star anise, and orange zest. Bring to a simmer, stirring gently, until the sugar dissolves. Add the pears and simmer gently for 25–30 minutes, turning them occasionally, until they are tender and take on a reddish hue. Remove the pears and set them on a plate. Reduce the spiced syrup in the pot for 15–20 minutes over low heat, until slightly thickened. Set aside.

Make the pavlovas: Preheat the oven to 230°F (110°C, convection). Line a baking sheet with parchment paper. In a medium bowl, combine the egg whites and 1 teaspoon of water and beat with the hand mixer to firm peaks. Gradually add the powdered sugar and vanilla sugar, continuing to beat for about 10 minutes, until glossy. Gently fold in the vinegar and cornstarch.

Use two spoons to dollop the meringue mixture onto the baking sheet, forming round shapes about 3 inches in diameter.

Bake the pavlovas for about 2 hours. After baking, turn off the oven and leave the pavlovas inside for 1 additional hour to dry out, occasionally opening the oven door to let steam escape. Once cooled, transfer the pavlovas to a wire rack.

Slice the marinated pears into fan shapes, keeping them attached at the stem, and serve each with a pavlova and a dollop of whipped cream. Drizzle some of the spiced syrup over the top and sprinkle with chopped pistachios for garnish.

Tip: Any leftover pavlovas can be stored in an airtight container for 1–2 weeks.

CRÊPES SUZETTE

THIS CLASSIC FRENCH DESSERT FEATURES DELICATE CRÊPES SERVED WITH A RICH ORANGE SAUCE, FLAMED WITH THE FINEST HIGHLAND WHISKY. FOR AN INDULGENT TOUCH, SERVE EACH CRÊPE WITH A SCOOP OF VANILLA ICE CREAM.

INGREDIENTS FOR 4 SERVINGS:

FOR THE CRÊPE BATTER:
2 cups (250 g) spelt flour (type 630) or all-purpose flour
Sea salt
2 cups (500 ml) whole milk, divided
3 large eggs
3 ½ tablespoons unsalted butter, melted
Zest of 1 blood orange

FOR THE FILLING:
10 tablespoons unsalted butter, at room temperature
Zest of 3 blood oranges
½ cup (60 g) powdered sugar

TO FINISH:
Unsalted butter, for the pan
4 zested blood oranges from above
4 tablespoons whisky, divided
Powdered sugar, for dusting

SPECIAL EQUIPMENT:
nonstick pan or crêpe pan
lighter/cooking torch

Make the crêpe batter: In a large bowl, combine the flour, a pinch of salt, and half the milk. Stir vigorously to avoid lumps. Gradually add the remaining milk. In a separate medium bowl, whisk the eggs and then mix them into the batter, along with the melted butter and orange zest. Cover the batter and let it rest for 1 hour at room temperature.

Supreme the blood oranges: Place the 4 zested blood oranges on a work surface. Trim off the top and bottom ends, then cut off the peel and pith of each orange to expose the flesh, following the shape of the fruit. Cut toward the center of the orange (along a membrane), and then slice along the adjacent membrane until an orange segment falls free. Place the segment in a medium bowl, and continue cutting until all the oranges have been segmented. Squeeze any remaining juice from the discarded parts of the oranges into the same bowl and set aside.

Make the filling: In a medium bowl, combine the butter, orange zest, and powdered sugar, and mix with a spatula until smooth and homogenous.

Cook the crêpes: In a nonstick pan over medium heat, melt a little butter. Ladle a thin layer of batter into the pan, tilting it to evenly coat the base. Cook, flipping once, until golden on both sides. Repeat until you have cooked about 8 crêpes, re-greasing the pan as needed.

Assemble the crêpes: Reserve half of the orange butter for flambéing. On a work surface or plate, spread the orange butter on one half of a crêpe, then fold it in half. Spread more orange butter on the folded crêpe, then fold it in half again. Repeat this process with the remaining crêpes.

Flambé: In a large deep skillet over medium heat, melt half of the reserved orange butter. Add 4 filled crêpes and half of the orange segments along with their juice. Heat gently and pour in 2 tablespoons of whisky. Carefully flambé by igniting the whisky (be cautious with this step). Repeat the process with the remaining crêpes and orange sections.

Serve 2 crêpes per dessert plate, dusted with a little powdered sugar.

Nut Bundt Cake, recipe on page 232 – FROST

NUT BUNDT CAKE

THIS AIRY LEAVENED NUT CAKE IS A LOVELY TREAT
THAT REMAINS WONDERFULLY MOIST FOR DAYS.

INGREDIENTS FOR 1 BUNDT CAKE:

———

14 tablespoons unsalted butter, at room temperature, plus more for greasing the bundt pan
¾ cup (150 g) light raw cane sugar
Seeds from ½ vanilla bean
4 large eggs, separated
1¼ cups (150 g) spelt flour (type 630) or all-purpose flour, plus more for dusting
1½ teaspoons baking powder
Ground Ceylon cinnamon
Ground cardamom
Ground cloves
Freshly grated nutmeg
1 cup (100 g) ground walnuts
1 cup (100 g) ground almonds
Sea salt
½ cup (100 g) Greek yogurt
Powdered sugar, for dusting (optional)

SPECIAL EQUIPMENT:
10-inch (26-cm) round Bundt pan; electric hand mixer

Preheat the oven to 350°F (180°C, convection). Grease the pan with softened or melted butter and lightly dust with flour. Invert the pan to shake off any excess flour.

In a large bowl, combine the butter, sugar, and vanilla seeds. Beat with the mixer until light and fluffy. Gradually add the egg yolks, mixing well after each addition.

In a separate medium bowl, combine the flour, baking powder, a pinch each of cinnamon, cardamom, cloves, and nutmeg, and the walnuts and almonds.

In another medium bowl, beat the egg whites with a pinch of salt to stiff peaks.

Gently fold ⅓ of the flour mixture, ⅓ of the whipped egg whites, and ⅓ of the yogurt into the butter mixture. Repeat this process with the remaining thirds, folding gently to maintain the airy texture.

Pour the batter into the prepared pan and smooth the top. Bake for 60 minutes, or until a toothpick inserted in the center comes out clean.

Allow the cake to cool in the pan for a few minutes before inverting it onto a wire rack to cool completely.

Dust with powdered sugar before serving, if desired.

TARTAN COOKIES

THESE CRISP OAT COOKIES ARE INSPIRED BY THE WONDERFUL
TARTAN PATTERNS WE DISCOVERED ALL OVER SCOTLAND.

**INGREDIENTS FOR ABOUT
50 COOKIES:**

FOR THE COOKIES:
¾ cup (60 g) rolled oats
¾ cup (100 g) spelt flour (type 630)
   or all-purpose flour
Sea salt
¼ cup (40 g) light raw cane sugar
6 tablespoons cold unsalted butter,
   cubed

FOR THE ICING:
1 small egg white
½ cup (60 g) powdered sugar
1 teaspoon lemon juice
Ground Ceylon cinnamon
Cocoa powder

SPECIAL EQUIPMENT:
food processor; square cookie
   cutter; electric hand mixer; small
   paintbrush

In a medium dry skillet over low heat, toast the oats until they are fragrant. Let them cool on a plate, then use the food processor to grind them into a fine flour.

In a large bowl, combine the oat flour, spelt flour, a pinch of salt, and the sugar. Add the butter, and quickly work it in with your hands until the mixture is crumbly. Form it into a dough.

Preheat the oven to 320°F (160°C, convection). Line 2 baking sheets with parchment paper.

Roll out the dough on a lightly floured surface to a ⅛-inch (3-mm) thickness. Slide an offset spatula or long thin knife under the dough to ensure it doesn't stick to the surface.

Use the cookie cutter to cut out the cookies. Place them on the baking sheets and chill for 30 minutes.

Bake the cookies for 13–14 minutes, until they are golden brown. Let them cool on a wire rack.

While the cookies bake/cool, in a small bowl, use the hand mixer to beat the egg white with the powdered sugar and lemon juice until smooth. To create different colors, mix cinnamon into one half and cocoa powder into the other half, a pinch at a time until you get the desired shade.

Use the paintbrush to paint decorative icing patterns on the cooled cookies. Allow the icing to dry before serving. Store any leftovers in an airtight container for up to 1 week.

FROST – *Tartan Cookies, recipe on page 233*

PINE-NEEDLE GIFT TOPPERS

THE WELSH ARTIST ROSA HARRADINE, WHO CRAFTS LARGE COLORFUL BROOMS AND BRUSHES FROM NATURAL FIBERS, INSPIRED US TO CREATE THESE WHIMSICAL TOPPERS FOR WRAPPED HOLIDAY GIFTS. BUNDLING AND WRAPPING THE PINE NEEDLES IS MEDITATIVE AND ENJOYABLE—IT'S AN ACTIVITY ENHANCED BY A CUP OF TEA AND SOME LOVELY MUSIC.

MATERIALS NEEDED:

Long needles from the ponderosa pine (*Pinus ponderosa*)
Scissors
Red hemp twine

For each topper, count out 21 pine needles and bundle them neatly. Hold the bundle together at the base end of the needles and tap the base lightly with the closed scissors to ensure they line up perfectly.

Now, start wrapping: Tie the hemp twine around the brown end of the needles and wrap it tightly around the bundle three times. Make sure the wrapping is neat and tight, as this is important for the appearance (Drawing 1).

Next, gently bend three needles away from the bundle and wrap the remaining needles three more times. Then, bend the next three needles away and wrap the rest again three times (Drawing 2). Continue wrapping this way until only three needles remain. Wrap them the same way and secure the twine with a knot.

Finally, use scissors to trim the bottom tips of the pine needles into a nice curve so the finished topper resembles a flat broom (Drawing 3). To attach the topper to a gift, simply thread a piece of hemp twine through the top. Beautiful!

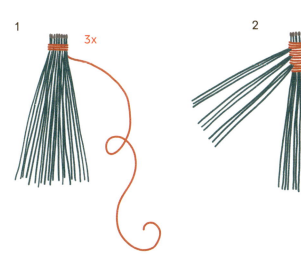

BLACKBERRY TRIFLE

THIS EYE-CATCHING DESSERT CAPTURES THE ESSENCE OF SCOTTISH WILD BLACKBERRIES AND MAKES A STUNNING CENTERPIECE FOR ANY GATHERING.

INGREDIENTS FOR 4 SERVINGS:

———

3 cups (450 g) fresh blackberries (or frozen and thawed), divided
¼ cup (50 g) powdered sugar
½ cup (50 g) flaked almonds
½ cup (50 g) rolled oats
2 tablespoons unsalted butter
¼ cup (50 g) honey
Generous ¾ cup (200 ml) heavy cream
1 cup (240 g) quark or Greek yogurt
2 teaspoons vanilla sugar or granulated sugar
Zest of ½ orange
1 tablespoon light raw cane sugar
½ cup (45 g) crumbled store-bought meringue

In a medium saucepan over medium heat, combine 2 cups (300 g) of the blackberries and the powdered sugar. Cook, stirring continuously, for about 3 minutes, until the sugar melts and the berries soften and start to release juices. Set aside to cool.

In a medium dry skillet over medium heat, toast the almond flakes and oats until aromatic. Add the butter and honey, bring to a brief boil, and then let the mixture cool on a plate.

In a large bowl, whip the cream to stiff peaks. Gently fold in the quark, vanilla sugar, orange zest, and raw cane sugar.

In a glass serving bowl, layer the ingredients as follows: start with ⅓ of the cream mixture, followed by ⅓ of the crumbled meringue, ⅓ of the cooked blackberries, ⅓ of the remaining fresh blackberries, and ⅓ of the oat mixture. Repeat this layering two more times.

ALMOND FRUITCAKE

THIS DELIGHTFUL CAKE IS PERFECT FOR A COZY TEATIME.

INGREDIENTS FOR 1 CAKE:

FOR THE CAKE:
- 1 cup (200 g) raisins
- ½ cup (100 ml) rum
- 12 tablespoons unsalted butter, at room temperature, plus more for the metal mold
- Sea salt
- ¾ cup (150 g) light raw cane sugar
- 4 large eggs, separated
- 2 ½ cups (300 g) spelt flour (type 630) or all-purpose flour
- 1 tablespoon baking powder
- 1 tablespoon whole milk
- ½ cup (60 g) candied lemon peel
- ½ cup (60 g) candied orange peel

FOR DECORATION:
- 1 cup (about 100 g) blanched almonds (see Tip)
- 1 tablespoon maple syrup
- Powdered sugar for dusting (optional)

SPECIAL EQUIPMENT:
- electric hand mixer; 7-inch (18-cm) paper or metal panettone mold

The day before, combine the raisins and rum in a bowl. Cover and let sit at room temperature overnight. The next day, drain the raisins and discard the rum.

Preheat the oven to 350°F (180°C, convection). If using a metal mold, grease it with butter. In a large bowl, combine the butter, a pinch of salt, and the sugar, and beat with the mixer until creamy and white. Slowly beat in the egg yolks.

Sift the flour and baking powder into a medium bowl. In a separate medium bowl, beat the egg whites to stiff peaks.

Gently fold half of the flour-baking powder mixture into the butter mixture. Gently stir in the milk. Add the drained raisins, candied lemon peel, and candied orange peel, and stir gently. Fold in the remaining flour and then the egg whites.

Place the panettone mold on a parchment-lined baking sheet. Pour the batter into the mold and decorate the top with the almonds. Bake for 60–65 minutes, until a skewer inserted in the middle of the cake comes out clean. (After about 40 minutes, you may need to cover the top of the cake with a piece of parchment paper to keep it from browning too much.)

Remove the cake from the oven and brush the top with maple syrup for a glossy finish. Transfer it to a wire rack to cool. (If you used a metal mold, carefully remove the cake from the mold before cooling.) If desired, dust with powdered sugar before serving. When well-wrapped and stored in a cool place, this cake stays fresh for 4–5 days.

Tip: Almonds can easily be blanched by pouring boiling water over them and letting them sit briefly. Then, using your thumb and forefinger, gently press the almonds out of their skins

ACKNOWLEDGEMENTS

Without my beloved family and their tremendous support, this book would not exist! Many thanks to my loved ones: my husband, Jean-Marc, and my children, Maxim, Léonore Mathilde, and Anson Carl. I will always remember our adventurous trips to Scotland and to the islands of Lewis and Harris in the Outer Hebrides. The captivating facets of the landscape, the warm-hearted people, and their vibrant traditions and craftsmanship keep drawing us back. To Lucia, my mother and co-author: I am so delighted to be able to work with you. Our shared love for tweed has fueled our hearts for so long. Now, with this book, a long-held dream has come true. To my father, Manfred: your expert support and tireless commitment to this project have once again been outstanding!

Anna, Marieke, and Insa: your remarkable dedication at Hazelnut House means so much to me, and your creative contributions to this book project will never be forgotten. Thank you also for the help on set, dear Reina. A huge thank you to all the wonderful people in Scotland who have always welcomed us with open arms: Gary from Ivybank Lodge, and Julia and her team at Wild Gorse. Emma, we will never forget your art tour and teatime at the Fife Arms Hotel. Nicola and John from Campbell's of Beauly Tweed Shop, Emily Scott from Knockando Woolmill, Michael Gates-Fleming from the Aberfeldy weaving mill, and designer Vixy Rae from Edinburgh—you all continue to inspire us with tweed.

And a thousand thanks to the best team! What incredible international female power, what creative energy! Melina, our shared journey as a dream team to the Scottish Highlands was unique and full of inspiration. Photoshoots with you are simply amazing! Julia, our collaboration is a firework of ideas. Your creativity and personal dedication touch us deeply. You have beautifully combined the images and texts into a unique work. Special thanks to you, dear Katharina, for all the illustrations and especially the enchanting map of Scotland. Magdalena, the editing process was a perfect collaboration. Thanks to the entire wonderful Brandstätter team!

A BIG THANK-YOU TO OUR PARTNERS

Kitchen appliances: Gaggenau

Earrings: Schwester Schwester

Tweed: Campbell's of Beauly Tweed Shop, Knockando Woolmill Tweed Museum, Glenlyon Tweed Mill, Wild Gorse Studio

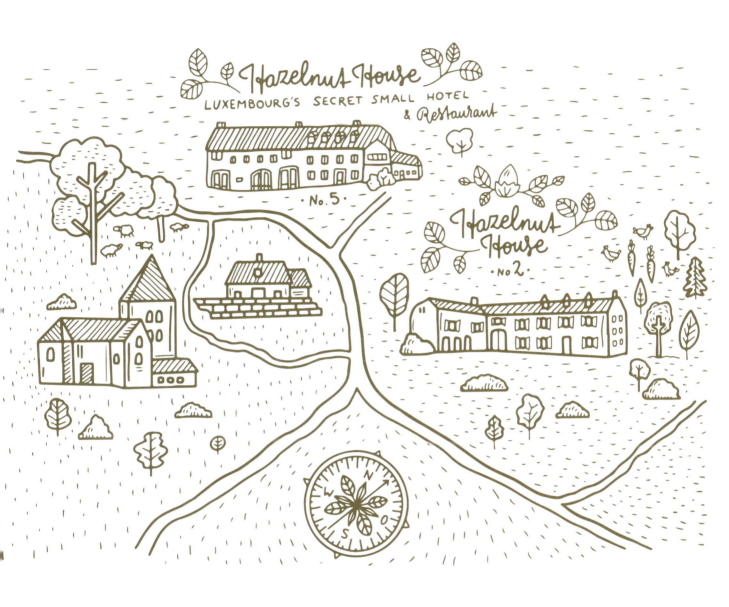

 THE WORLD OF HAZELNUT HOUSE

welcome@hazelnut-house.com

www.hazelnut-house.com

RECIPES *(in alphabetical order by ingredient)*

A

Almond Fruitcake 243
Apple Caramel Cheesecake 28
Apple Toffee Cake 17
Fall **Apple** Tart 26

B

Beet Dumplings with Brown Butter 59
Blackberry Trifle 240
Borscht 56
Butternut Squash-Potato Gratin 85
Caramelized **Butternut Squash** Tart 76
Pasta with Roasted **Butternut Squash** 80
Vanilla **Butter** Brioche 32

C

Castle **Cookie** Box 189
Cauliflower-Almond Soup 63
Cheese Soufflé with a Fresh Field Salad 164
Cinnamon Wreath 170
Crêpes Suzette 228
Roasted **Cauliflower** and Potatoes with Tahini Sauce 67
Tartan **Cookies** 233
Whole Roasted **Cauliflower** 68

F

Fig Confit 118
Fish & Chips 167

G

Grapefruit Rosemary Ale 179

H

"**Hazelnut** House" **Hazelnut** Cake 196
Hazelnut Zwieback 222

K

Kale Salad with Baked Goat Cheese 62

L

Leek Quiche 46
Roasted **Leeks** with Lentil Topping 47

M

Fall **Mushroom** Pizza 97
Fall **Mushroom** Soup 101
Mushroom and Chestnut Pie 93
Pan-Seared **Mackerel** with Celery-Apple Salad 14
Pasta with **Mushrooms** 102

N

Nut Bundt Cake 232
Scottish **Nut** Roast Balls with Jeweled Rice 159

O

"Dunkeld" Overnight **Oats** 142
Oaties 151
Red **Onions** in Puff Pastry 41

P

Autumn Cup **Pumpkin** Soup 71
Focaccia with **Potatoes** and Onions 86
Pavlovas with Poached **Pears** 226
Pear Tart 23
Pears and Brussels Sprouts with Potato-Celery Mash 163
Plum Tart 123
Potato Dumplings with Apple Sauerkraut 52
Butternut Squash-**Potato** Gratin 85

Q

Quince-Orange Jam 36

R

Rice Pudding with Cinnamon-Roasted Figs 116
Rose Hip Jelly 35

S

Highlands **Scones** 174
Homemade **Sauerkraut** 51
"Oh Deer" Fine Scottish **Shortbread** 131
Salmon with a Crunchy Crust and Root Mash 160
Spice-Cured **Salmon** 152
Spiced **Shortbread** Leaves 221

W

Spelt **Walnut** Bread 175

RECIPES *(by category)*

SEASONAL SOUPS

Autumn Cup Pumpkin Soup 71

Borscht 56

Cauliflower-Almond Soup 63

Fall Mushroom Soup 101

VEGETARIAN DISHES

Beet Dumplings with Brown Butter 59

Caramelized Butternut Squash Tart 76

Cheese Soufflé with a Fresh Field Salad 164

Fall Mushroom Pizza 97

Homemade Sauerkraut 51

Kale Salad with Baked Goat Cheese 62

Leek Quiche 46

Mushroom and Chestnut Pie 93

Pasta with Mushrooms 102

Pasta with Roasted Butternut Squash 80

Pears and Brussels Sprouts with Potato-Celery Mash 163

Potato Dumplings with Apple Sauerkraut 52

Butternut Squash-Potato Gratin 85

Roasted Cauliflower and Potatoes with Tahini Sauce 67

Roasted Leeks with Lentil Topping 47

Scottish Nut Roast Balls with Jeweled Rice 159

Whole Roasted Cauliflower 68

FISH DISHES

Fish & Chips 167

Pan-Seared Mackerel with Celery-Apple Salad 14

Salmon with a Crunchy Crust and Root Mash 160

Spice-Cured Salmon 152

HEAVENLY DESSERTS

Blackberry Trifle 240

Crêpes Suzette 228

Pavlovas with Poached Pears 226

Rice Pudding with Cinnamon-Roasted Figs 116

FOR A FALL PICNIC

Fall Apple Tart 26

Focaccia with Potatoes and Onions 86

Highlands Scones 174

Leek Quiche 46

Mushroom and Chestnut Pie 93

Pear Tart 23

Plum Tart 123

Red Onions in Puff Pastry 41

Spelt Walnut Bread 175

Vanilla Butter Brioche 32

CAKES AND TARTS

Almond Fruitcake 243

Apple Caramel Cheesecake 28

Apple Toffee Cake 17

Fall Apple Tart 26

"Hazelnut House" Hazelnut Cake 196

Nut Bundt Cake 232

Pear Tart 23

Plum Tart 123

PASTRIES AND BREADS

Cinnamon Wreath 170

Focaccia with Potatoes and Onions 86

Highlands Scones 174

Spelt Walnut Bread 175

Vanilla Butter Brioche 32

SUNDAY BREAKFAST

Cinnamon Wreath 170

"Dunkeld" Overnight Oats 142

Highlands Scones 174

Nut Bundt Cake 232

Quince-Orange Jam 36

Rose Hip Jelly 35

Spelt Walnut Bread 175

Vanilla Butter Brioche 32

TEATIME COOKIES

Castle Cookie Box 189

Hazelnut Zwieback 222

Oaties 151

"Oh Deer" Fine Scottish Shortbread 131

Spiced Shortbread Leaves 221

Tartan Cookies 233

APPETIZING INVITATIONS

Fall Mushroom Pizza 97

Fig Confit 118

Focaccia with Potatoes and Onions 86

Grapefruit Rosemary Ale 179

Oaties 151

Red Onions in Puff Pastry 41

Spice-Cured Salmon 152

CRAFTING AND HANDIWORK

Magical Fan Garland 225

Napkin Ring for a Fall Dinner 210

Pine-Needle Gift Toppers 239

Papier-Mâché Lanterns 125

Stamp Workshop 43

"Tweed Time" Bookmark 113

POETRY

"Morning" 218

"My Heart's in the Highlands" 136

"September Morning" 74

TEAM

THERESA BAUMGÄRTNER, *Concept, Text, Recipes, Photos, Food Styling, Set Styling*

Born in 1987 in Hamburg, Germany, Theresa Baumgärtner now lives with her family in Luxembourg. After completing her master's degree in culture and economics, she followed her heart professionally: Today, she is a successful cookbook author, writes and photographs for magazines, and works as a freelance television presenter. At Hazelnut House, her guesthouse in the east of Luxembourg, she celebrates seasonal and regional cuisine as well as delightfully romantic decorations in her workshops. Follow her and Hazelnut on Instagram as she shares insights on kitchen, garden, and table culture: @hazelnut_house_1851.

www.theresaskueche.de
www.hazelnut-house.com

LUCIA BAUMGÄRTNER, *Concept, Text, Recipes*

Born in 1962 in northern Baden, Germany, Lucia Baumgärtner now lives south of Hamburg and has been working as a freelance writer for many years. Her enthusiasm for culinary topics is evident in her work and cookbooks.

MELINA KUTELAS, *Photography*

After several years as a fashion stylist in London, Melina Kutelas changed fields and has since worked as a freelance food photographer and stylist. Since 2015, she has run the food blog *About that Food*, which served as a springboard for her culinary career. In 2017, she was awarded the Austria Food Blog Award for her food styling. She lives and works in Vienna.

www.melinakutelas.com

KATHARINA RALSER, *Illustrations*

Born in Vorarlberg, Austria, Katharina studied graphic design in Vienna and Paris. Always searching for the ideal forms for her projects, she experiments with many techniques.

www.katharinaralser.at

Highland Harvest was first published in the United States by Tra Publishing, 2025.

U.S. Edition Publisher & Creative Director
Ilona Oppenheim

U.S. Edition Art Director & Cover Design
Jefferson Quintana

U.S. Edition Editorial Director
Lisa McGuinness

U.S. Edition Publishing Director
Jessica Faroy

U.S. Edition Senior Designer
Morgane Leoni

Highland Harvest was first published by Christian Brandstätter Verlag GmbH & Co., in 2023 under the title *Tweed Time*.

Concept, Texts & Recipes
Theresa Baumgärtner

Art Direction, Concept, Texts & Recipes
Lucia Baumgärtner

Photographs
Melina Kutelas

Art Direction & Graphic Design
Julia Leissing

Illustrations & Craft Instructions
Katharina Ralser

Photography Credits:
Photograph on page 247: Ramunas Astrauskas
Photographs on pages 15, 18, 30, 72, 107, 214, 216, 219, 231, 234, 236, 244: Theresa Baumgärtner
Illustrations on pages 246, 248: Wald & Schwert Studio
Endpapers/Notes on pages 9, 127, 215: iStock Photo

We thank the rights holders for their kind permission to print the following poems:
Eduard Mörike: translated from "Septembermorgen" from Die schönsten Gedichte, Insel Verlag 1999
Christian Morgenstern: translated from "Morgen" from Gedichte in einem Band, Insel Verlag 2004
Robert Burns: "My Heart's in the Highlands" from Classic Scottish Poems, selected by Gaby Morgan, Macmillan Collector's Library 2021.

All rights reserved. No part of this book may be reproduced or transmitted in any form or by any means (electronic or mechanical, including photocopying, recording or any information retrieval system) without permission in writing from the publisher.

Printed and bound in China by Artron Art Co., Ltd.

This product is made of FSC ®- certified and other controlled material.

Tra Publishing is committed to sustainability in its materials and practices.

ISBN: 978-1-962098-30-4

Tra Publishing
245 NE 37th Street
Miami, FL 33137
trapublishing.com

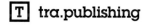

1 2 3 4 5 6 7 8 9 10